The Political Vocation of Philosophy

The Political Vocation of Philosophy

Donatella Di Cesare

Translated by David Broder

polity

Originally published in Italian as *Sulla vocazione politica della filosofia* © 2018
Bollati Boringhieri editore, Turin

This English edition © 2021 by Polity Press

Polity Press
65 Bridge Street
Cambridge CB2 1UR, UK

Polity Press
101 Station Landing
Suite 300
Medford, MA 02155, USA

ISBN-13: 978-1-5095-3941-3 - hardback
ISBN-13: 978-1-5095-3942-0 - paperback

A catalogue record for this book is available from the British Library.

Library of Congress Cataloging-in-Publication Data

Names: Di Cesare, Donatella, author. | Broder, David, translator.
Title: The political vocation of philosophy / Donatella Di Cesare ;
    translated by David Broder.
Other titles: Sulla vocazione politica della filosofia. English
Description: English edition. | Medford, MA : Polity Press, 2021. |
    "Originally published in Italian as Sulla vocazione politica della
    filosofia, 2018 Bollati Boringhieri editore, Torino." | Includes
    bibliographical references and index. | Summary: "This book seeks to
    redefine the purpose of philosophy for our times. Faced with the
    saturated immanence of the world, philosophy is summoned to return to
    its original vocation and, after a long absence in which it lost its
    voice, it is called on to reawaken the community and protect the life we
    share in common"-- Provided by publisher.
Identifiers: LCCN 2020041699 (print) | LCCN 2020041700 (ebook) | ISBN
    9781509539413 (hardback) | ISBN 9781509539420 (paperback) | ISBN
    9781509539437 (epub)
Subjects: LCSH: Political science--Philosophy. | Philosophy.
Classification: LCC JA71 .D48213 2021 (print) | LCC JA71 (ebook) | DDC
    320.01--dc23
LC record available at https://lccn.loc.gov/2020041699
LC ebook record available at https://lccn.loc.gov/2020041700

Typeset in 11 on 13pt Sabon by
Servis Filmsetting Ltd., Stockport, Cheshire
Printed and bound in Great Britain by Short Run Press

For further information on Polity, visit our website: politybooks.com

Contents

[P]hilosophy should not prophesy, but then again it should not remain asleep.

Martin Heidegger[1]

So our city will be governed by us and you with waking minds, and not as most cities now which are inhabited and ruled darkly as in a dream.

Plato[2]

[1] Martin Heidegger, *The Basic Problems of Phenomenology*, Bloomington: Indiana University Press, 1988, p. 178.
[2] Plato, *Republic*, 520c, trans. Paul Shorey.

1

The saturated immanence of the world

There's no longer an outside. Or at least, that's what the final stage of globalisation looks like. Up till the modern era, the inhabitants of the earth star meditated on the cosmos, turning their eyes to the open sky in admiration, amazement, wonder. The cosmos's boundless face was, nonetheless, a shelter, for it protected them from the absolute exteriority to which they felt exposed. Yet, when the planet was explored far and wide – circumnavigated, occupied, connected, depicted – a tear opened up in the cosmic sky, and the abyss opened up above them. Their gaze got lost in the icy outside.

This was an unprecedented challenge. The invention of the globe was the history of a 'spatio-political alienation'.[1] The external exercised a magnetic force, simultaneously both attracting and repelling; it was the otherness that had to be reduced, dominated, controlled. Even in that era, there were philosophical models. The cosmic-speculative sphere which had long inspired conjecture, intuition, ideas, was supplanted by the Copernican revolution. Thanks to this revolution – in which even the furthest limits fell one after another – anthropocentrism was proclaimed with great energy. Through complicated rotations and oscillations, the wandering star pursued this course for centuries – but without being able to escape its fate.

At the dawn of the third millennium, globalisation can be considered complete. It has proven to be the ultimate result of an uninterrupted monologue conducted by the world's propulsive force – a force majeure, an unstoppable force, almost a principle of reason. All grounds for criticism would thus prove superfluous. One can analyse the global situation. But no more than that. For the first time, philosophy would appear to have been checkmated by the axiom of actuality.

How can there be philosophy in a world without an outside? An attentive diagnosis will find that the globe's ontological regime is that of a saturated immanence. Immanence ought to be understood in the etymological sense of that which remains, which persists as itself, always within, without an outside, without exteriority. A static, compact immanence: there are neither splits nor voids, neither escape routes nor ways out. This is a spatial and temporal saturation.

This may be surprising. For is this not the world of absolute flows, of capital, of technology, of media? Information, fusion, density follow the convulsive beat of a dizzying acceleration. And, indeed, all this takes place under the sign of inevitable progress. But this is merely the semblance of a world trapped in the whirling economy of time, whose very essence paradoxically relies on speed.[2] The flows of the global web mark out the same orbits, following an ever-identical and repetitive movement. It is not that there is any lack of chaotic spirals, of tumultuous swirls. But they do not upset the constant rhythm of these absolute flows, which is irremovably fixed, secretly immobile. Speed collapses into stasis, acceleration ends up in inertia. It is like running on a treadmill in order to avoid slipping backward. Everything changes – yet, fundamentally, nothing truly does. Inertial change is the brand of the synchronised globe.

'Saturated immanence' refers to the asphyxial present of a world which, basing itself on the belief that it cannot be harmed, claims to have immunised itself against the 'outside'.[3] Thus it has swallowed up, banished, destroyed, all that is other to itself. It is driven to do this by an over-bearing immunological impulse: namely, the impulse to remain intact, to go on and on, whole and unscathed. All the negative powers have been summoned up in order to combat vital negativity, to pre-empt any change, to shoo away any alteration, to neutralise any loss. The immunological impulse was there in the past, too. But today, thanks to technology, it has discovered unprecedented forms.[4] In its saturated immanence, the globe of absolute flows is a monument to this impulse.

What's the point of foraying into the glacial, deathly beyond? Even to pose the question is the victory of exophobia – an abyssal fear, a cold panic, horror for whatever is external. This angst grips and stifles thought. How could one imagine any alternative? Any taking of distance, any interruption, is passed off as vain and impossible, even before it starts being denounced as a terrorist threat. One can dream only *internally*, within the regime of saturated immanence, in which dreams often transform into nightmares. The bitter acknowledgement that 'There is no longer an outside' has coloured even the most radical thought of recent years.[5] Thus the hyperrealist refrain 'There is no alternative!' – the mocking and sorrowful *summa* of the present era – has ended up as a cruel and incessantly realised prophecy.

It is no mystery that the discourse on the 'end of the world' is taken so seriously.[6] Such discourse takes its cue above all from the empirical sciences: climatology, geophysics, oceanography, biochemistry, ecology. Humanity's fall into catastrophe seems imminent. The near future – unforeseeable because it is completely other – is instead consigned to the scenarios portrayed in filmic drama or messianic visions. The Promethean cry risks being suffocated in an apocalyptic death-rattle. What is, at least, clear is that the late-capitalist world is the world of planet-wide ecological collapse. The fusion between techno-economy and biosphere is plain for all to see.[7]

'Anthropocene' is the name for that geological epoch in which humans look on near-impotently at the devastating and deadly effects of this asymmetrical fusion, in which nature has been eroded to the point of disappearance. Yet, the violence of this intrusion would not have been possible without the implacable, incandescent sovereignty of capital. But, in the contemporary imaginary, it seems easier to imagine the end of the world than the end of capitalism. Here lies the enormous discrepancy between scientific understanding and political impotence. At this point, capitalism has occupied the entire horizon of the thinkable. And it has done so by absorbing every hotbed of resistance within the imagination, by erasing every exteriority prior or posterior to its own history. It is as if before capitalism there was only the gloom of the archaic; after it, only the darkness of the apocalypse.

For humanity trapped in saturated immanence – in that windowless globe of advanced-stage capitalism, where very little human remains – it is, nonetheless, possible to conceive of a 'transhumanism'. This is the latest techno-gnostic dream of immortality, whether it is to be realised through cryogenic hibernation or by transferring identity into software. This is a dream yearned for by a species which could disappear at a stroke. May the posthuman survive, at least!

Internally, everything is supposed to be possible – but outside, nothing is. The question should then be posed of what 'possible' and 'impossible' mean, if in the techno-scientific context – even the most futuristic one – there is no limit that holds, while in the political context all prospect of change is precluded *a priori* by the 'No' put up by the market.[8] You can become immortal, but you cannot escape capitalism.

The world of saturated immanence is the world of the global-capitalist regime, the claustrophobic space oscillating between the non-event – the steady flows of liberal democracy – and the imminent planetary collapse. As the different fronts take form they divide those who look to a hyperbolic acceleration that would bring capitalism to self-destruction, from those who hope to stop the speeding locomotive by pulling the emergency brake.[9] After the Apocalypse, the Kingdom.

Capitalist realism reiterates the immanence and reinforces the closure.[10] Only a logic of the impossible would be able to deviate and dislocate it. To pre-empt the future in order to avoid it: the regime of saturated immanence is the closed world of a preventative police, a temporal prison where farsightedness crosses over into a clairvoyance that tries to ward off any change. This world has already escaped its shadow. It is condemned to the imperative of the day, to the exhausted torpor of the extended alarm, to the tireless half-sleep of a light that never goes out, in a diurnal virtuality that knows no night.

2

Heraclitus, wakefulness and the original communism

Since its debut, philosophy has paid particular attention to the theme of wakefulness, to the point that wakefulness becomes the symbolic representation, the perspicuous metaphor, that preceded philosophy even before it had a name. Wakefulness is the mysterious surging of an inner light that marks a re-emergence from the night. It is the force of being re-summoned, the wonder of the life that stands up again, the return to the self. Philosophy is, first of all, this.

It was Heraclitus who separated the flaring of the day from myth, setting it up as a metaphysical category. He was called 'the obscure' because of his enigmatic and oracular style. Thus began the adventure of thought guided by the light of the *lógos*. It articulates the world, which becomes cosmos, unfolding in an uninterrupted transcendence of its own narrow, meagre range, toward an ever more vast, elevated and common sphere.

Very little is known about Heraclitus' life. Ancient biographers attributed him a royal descent. Diogenes Laërtius says that 'He was above all men of a lofty and arrogant spirit.'[1] This almost disdainful attitude owed to a dispute with his fellow citizens, whom he sharply rebuked for the exile imposed on his friend Hermodorus after the failed democratic revolution. Ephesus, an Ionian city at the border between the Turkish coast and the European sea, was not yet Athenian. But there was no lack of tensions. Resentful, Heraclitus distanced himself from political life and rejected the request to lay down laws for the *pólis*, which he now considered governed by a bad Constitution. He retired to the temple of Artemides, where, as legend has it, he set down his great book, subdivided into three discourses: the first on everything, the second on politics, and the third on theology. Someone later gave this work a title which entered into widespread use: *Perì phúseos*. It is almost as if Heraclitus had written a treatise on *phúsis*, on nature understood as the principle and substance of all things. Aristotle helped to entrench this vision – a misleading and reductive one. Yet there also exists an ancient tradition, further embodied by the Stoic Diodotus, according to whom Heraclitus' book had nothing to do with nature, except at a few points, and instead focused on political themes: *perì politeías*.

Moreover, it is not hard to recognise, against the numinous backdrop, the political-tragic inspiration of Heraclitus' thought in the over 120 extant fragments of his work. The man who speaks here is not so much the explorer of the cosmos as the severe guardian of the city, the interpreter of the *pólemos* – that conflict, the 'father' of all things, which reigns over everything (B 53). The quarrel in the *pólis* is projected onto all reality in order to scrutinise the foundations of the law that governs it, to connect together in its unity all that is apparently scattered and multiple, to grasp the *palíntropos harmoníe*, the 'discordant harmony' of opposites (B 51). The city offers the paradigm for interpreting the world.

Perceiving the one in everything that is differentiated: this is the great merit of Heraclitus, recognised as the forerunner of the dialectic. As Hegel wrote: 'Here we see land; there is no proposition of Heraclitus which I have not adopted in my Logic.'[2] Yet, one should avoid any distortion of historical perspective here. The harmony of opposites – the enigmatic bond of which Heraclitus speaks – is not a speculative unity, but rather the unexpected passage through which the one incessantly changes into the other: life and death, day and night, wakefulness and sleep, summer and winter, peace and war. This vision has wrongly been ossified in a doctrine of perennial becoming, of fluidity, that *pánta rheî* of which there is no trace in the fragments from Heraclitus. He does, indeed, speak of the river 'we enter and do not enter, we are and we are not' (B 49a) – but only in order to emphasise the constant replacement of its ever-different waters. Unsurprisingly, it is the flame – which survives by transforming itself, which changes depending on the airs with which it mixes – that visually renders the harmonious concord among opposites.

Nothing can escape this law, not even the names which shed light on oppositions. Heraclitus was first in that line-up of thinkers who looked to language in order to understand reality. The hidden harmony which governs the cosmos is harboured within the *lógos*, which everything must happen in accordance with. This is an eternal and universal law, able to regulate becoming, which is not a blind plunge but rather a knowing move back and forth, from one opposite to the other.

But who will want to listen to the *lógos*? Who will want to listen to it, in its enigmatic ambiguity? This is Heraclitus' question – and it already contains a warning. Deaf, absent, almost numbed, prey to flows of dreams and particular opinions – far from what is 'wise', *sóphon* – mortals draw away from listening. They live closed in on themselves, as if they were dreaming, prisoners of their own private existence, of their suffocating small-mindedness. Hence the denunciation of idiocy, which in Greek is etymologically related to property – *idiótes* derives from *ídios*, 'one's own'. It is, then, impossible to reach what is 'common', *koinón*. Heraclitus uses the Ionian form *xunón*, which through a play on words arrives at *xùn nôi*, that is, at *noûs*, 'with reason' (B 114). Not only is intelligence common, but that which is common is based on intelligence. This is not a matter of immediate intuition, but rather of the knowledge that orders the cosmos, which is articulated and combined in the *lógos*. An idiot is he who refuses to listen, who remains in the isolation of the night, cutting himself off from participation in the common day and the common world. Thus rings out the sentence passed by Heraclitus: 'The waking have one common world, but the sleeping turn aside each into a world of his own' (B 89).

As night and day follow one after the other, they beat the rhythm of time; but unlike what Hesiod imagined, they are not separate. Rather, they are a single whole, even if they alternate as opposites. But neither passes over into the other – for they remain distinct. Night and day point beyond themselves: they are indices, or rather symbols. The oppositions multiply. While the ultimate polarity of life and death appears enigmatically in the background – will there be a return, from death to life? – darkness and light summon sleep and wakefulness. The first metaphysician of light, Heraclitus represented the day as wisdom spreading out from the *lógos*, which makes common in the light. Wakefulness is the prelude to philosophy.

The call to wakefulness recurs constantly throughout the fragments.[3] Philosophy would subsequently make this exhortation its own. To think is to have a part in keeping vigilance over the *lógos* which makes common. 'Private wisdom', *idía phrónesis*, is an oxymoron, because that which arises in the individual – dreams, images, opinions, ideas – is but an empty, dead illusion. This illusion is destined to persist so long as it does not find the path of commonality. So no, do not sleep! Do not let yourselves be carried off by the sleep of private idiocy! Heraclitus repeated this exhortation, directed at the many who lived in torpor. As his peremptory injunction has it: 'It is wrong to act and speak like men asleep' (B 73). But there's sleep, and then there's sleep. Healthy, restorative sleep is good.

Yet, it is an error to mistake day for night, to confuse wakefulness with sleep, when what distinguishes them is that suddenness which, like a darting flame, ratifies the mysterious passage between opposites.

For Heraclitus, this is even more true for wakefulness than it is for sleep. Whoever sleeps, though remaining the same person, seems to be another, *ergátas*, the 'artifice' of a world of his own (B 75). He resembles a dead man lying there, inert and distant. In one abstruse fragment, passed down by Clement of Alexandria, it is said, 'Man kindles a light for himself in the night-time, when he has died but is alive. The sleeper, whose vision has been put out, lights up from the dead; he that is awake lights up from the sleeping' (B 26). Whoever gives in to sleep abandons the *koinón*, the common world, to plunge into his own world, where he lies with the dead. Sleep is like a brief descent into Hades, in the gloomy underworld beneath the city. Thus, the citizen who sleeps is not only apathetic and alogical, but also apolitical and anomic. He ceases, rather, to be a citizen; he unites with its dead in the private burial recess which is, at the same time, the tomb of the public. He twists and turns in his illusions, in his nightmares, in his imagination, in his hallucinations. When it is night in the city and the world seems to sink away, perhaps no one is left to watch, alert, over the *pólis*. Yet there is one exception, or perhaps two. For there is both the wise god who keeps watch over the city walls, and his vicarious adept, the philosopher, who attentively surveils the city from within, so that this brightly lit opening does not forever close down in a private idiocy.

Is politics, then, the daughter of philosophy? The philosopher combats the night's tendency to reduce everything to nothing. And even if one day everyone should give in, the city would remain, conserved in the thought of this extraordinary and attentive citizen.

The guardian of the city even before Plato and his *politéia*, Heraclitus denounces the political night. He points an accusing finger against the sleepwalking so widespread among his co-citizens, who do not want to wake up even during the day. He speaks of 'night-walkers', *nuktipóloi*, who hang out at – and with – night rather than lead the life required by the common day of the city. Heraclitus' words are inspired by sarcasm, disappointment and disdain; his diurnal *lógos* inaugurates the space of the Greek *pólis* and, more generally, the ambit of European politics. The city can exist only thanks to the *koinón*, the common, gathered in the *lógos*. This is the ordering intelligence which guarantees the *nómos* on which the city bases itself. The diurnal *lógos* exposes the *pólis*'s very existence; it heralds political ontology. 'Those who speak with understanding must hold fast to what is common to all as a city holds fast to its law, and even more strongly' (B 114).

In short: without the *koinón* of the *lógos* there is no *pólis*. Without the link provided by the *lógos*, which is common and makes common, the city could not come to pass. What maintains the unity of the citizens is the *koinón*, their participation in the day, beyond the isolation of the night. And this is why the return to the self comes through the re-entry into the political space. The original communism of vigilance – of which philosophy becomes the guardian – is the condition of political existence.

3

The narcosis of light: on the night of capital

The metaphysics of light have followed a long journey in the West, leading from the common wakefulness to an exclusive and systematic knowledge. This is an unstoppable re-formation of the day, which expands and dilates to become much more than a simple interval between two nights. The dark areas are reduced, while the continuum of certainty illuminates all things in a whole of crystalline self-evidence. There is nothing, or almost nothing, that universal Reason does not unveil and bring out into the open. Thus, it decrees the triumph of the explicit over the concealed, of the present over the absent. What is no more, or not yet, degrades to a mere no-thing, by way of a stubborn ontology that chases away all otherness.

With a renewed Promethean endeavour, one can attempt to glimpse the perpetual light of the world beyond, in order to translate it – down here – into a constant enlightenment. This latter maintains the same uniform intensity without ever lighting up or going out. This is a decisive response – and it claims to be a definitive one – to the *pavor nocturnus* which has shaken the history of the world over the centuries. Better a narcosis of light, as a pre-emptive measure against the imminent apocalypse.

In the Book of Revelation, it is said: 'And the city had no need of the sun, neither of the moon . . . the gates of it shall not be shut at all by day: for there shall be no night there' (21, 23–5 KJV). The fight against concealed powers reached its peak in the modernity of the age of Lights. Then, it was put on pause when, rather than incriminate the night, the first Romantics lamented its loss. In his *Hymns*, Novalis proclaimed the night 'holy, ineffable, mysterious'.[1] The night is the robust ally of that interiority which otherwise threatens to vanish. But then this fight resumed its onward march, now with an accelerated rhythm, guided by science and underpinned by technology, which promised to do battle to the last against darkness. Metaphysical lights took concrete form and became electrical installations. The city, floodlit by the positive thought which guaranteed a pragmatic way of life, could forget the night. Or, better, mindful of what the Romantics had warned, it could recover the night, entrusting whatever was left of it to psychoanalysis's field of competence. The overcoming of the night decreed and ratified the victory of the day which aspires to become permanent, expanding in a circadian continuum.

What would Heraclitus have said about this metaphysical illusionism, which transforms night into day, takes away opposites and erases the pulse and rhythm of the ancient cycle of sleep and wakefulness? Certainly, he would not have applauded all this. He dreaded the political night, with its capacity to disintegrate the communism of vigilance. But he would not have been inclined to approve that narcotic light which brings only sleepwalking and not high alert. For sure, he could not have imagined hundreds of millions of individuals sat up at night in front of bright screens, with such magnetic powers of attraction, which would forever compromise their imagination – meaning, that sublime human faculty of dreaming eyes-open, of losing oneself in one's own thoughts.

They call it 24/7 – the concept of time bent to boundless production and consumption, imposed by the market system. It refers to the non-stop, ceaseless industriousness that stretches out over twenty-four hours a day, seven days a week. Only through a willing, mocking ambiguity does it refer to weeks at all. For on closer inspection, 24/7 repudiates any rhythm, erases any scansion of time.[2] If the globe aims to be always-operational, why should human existence not itself adapt to this?

It would be mistaken to confuse 24/7 with modernity's desolate rush into homogeneity, as critiqued by Lukács, Benjamin and others at the dawn of the twentieth century. For that time still had its rhythm set by the agenda of progress, linked to the illusion of growth. 24/7 is the time-without-becoming of post-history, the permanent day, capitalism's final mirage. And fundamentally, such an outcome was part of its plans.

This was true already with the first electric city lights, a guarantee of security and a projection of success. The intense, brilliant lighting which spread across the universal supermarket seemed to fulfil this initial promise. The fight against darkness, blackness, the shadows, phantasms, mystery, the unknown, is the paroxysmal result of a stubborn and prolonged Enlightenment spirit which opened up a new sky: an atmosphere of disaster. Blanchot has emphasised the etymology of disaster:[3] an expanse without stars, without the points of reference which would allow one to orient oneself. Even if there were stars, they would no longer be visible, for they are hidden by the artificial lighting that never turns off. Under that empty sky, the planetary shopping mall continues its tireless operations with its infinite variety of offers.

No obstacle seems to hold back the 24/7, if not human fragility itself. Capitalism eliminates all difference: between sacred and profane, between mechanical and organic. Already in his time, Karl Marx grasped this violent bid to knock down natural barriers. The 24/7 abolishes the boundary between light and darkness, day and night, activity and rest. Sleep, then, seems to be an out-right affront to the incessant industriousness the market imposes; it appears an undue resistance to the adaptation which digital networks demand. The planet has sped up the pace, projecting itself, exultant, toward the non-stop – and existence ought to be no exception to this.

So, what is sleep, this 'outside' the world, this dark retreat from existence, in which the world itself pulls back, disappears for a bit, takes a pause? No, the long night of capital, lit up like daytime, cannot allow any pause, any absence. Especially because acosmia – the world's temporary escape – is, at the same time, an illegitimate flight from the world, a dangerous interruption, an anomaly of the individual existence which, even just by sleeping, tacitly stands opposed to the law of the planetary non-stop.

It cannot be granted that sleep is a natural necessity. For that would be to accept this vast quantity of time being wasted, hours and hours lost in an irrecuperable void, from which no profit is drawn. All the other human needs – hunger, thirst, sex drive, not to mention love and friendship – have been reviewed and proposed in commodified versions. Hence this process must finally affect even sleep, the final frontier of human finitude. In open contrast with the 24/7 universe, sleep seems all the more scandalous – both because it is the trace of an almost pre-modern era which ought to have been overcome already, but also because it is the body's tie to the alternation of light and dark, beating the rhythm of activity and rest. This is the alternation which capitalism wants to erase or, at least, neutralise.

This is visible also when one takes in the full sweep of the transhumanist project. This project no longer accepts unalterable natural givens; it takes every barrier for a challenge and has declared war even on the ultimate limit – death. For transhumanism, sleep becomes almost a new pathology, to be eradicated with new substances. It does so even if only to have the advantage of more time, which is ever more lacking in the third-millennium life-form. The attack on sleep thus seems almost legitimate.

Insomnia is a chronic condition for the inhabitants of the extra-temporal 24/7 universe – this routine of the always-the-same, the intensely illuminated artificial environment. This is not, however, only a matter of the insomnia caused by an alert wakefulness, full to the brim with responsibilities. It does not spring from the refusal to overlook – in the oblivion of sleep – the violence that shakes the world. It is not born of worry for the pain of others, of impotence in the face of disaster – as Levinas masterfully described.[4] The appropriate term for this new insomnia is sleep-mode – that is, the setting for some technological device which is neither off nor on. It is sleep in a deferred or reduced form, harbouring a constant alertness made visible by the dim light of the screen. Into the darkness it insinuates a time protected from the night. Here prevails a lack of sensitivity, a denial of memory, a limiting of the faculties of perception, the impossibility of reflection. It is a prolonged trance state, a mass sleepwalking. In this almost inert half-sleep, in this pervasive torpor, is it possible to wake up again?

4

The *pólis*: a calling

Rather than give a classic definition of philosophy, this book prefers to interrogate its intemporal element, put to the test by the demands of the time. This means that it proposes a political-existential reflection, or better, an existential and political reflection, on philosophy's fate, on its role, on its potential in the era of technocapitalism and neoliberal governance.

Philosophy has always been harried, attracted, cajoled by two ruinous temptations. The first is that of closing in on itself, abstracting itself completely from the world. The second is that of completely casting off its own self, becoming absolutely other. Given that this has always happened, it would be bizarre to get carried away by assertions of 'unprecedented' developments. But these two temptations are today being conjugated in a double closure, perhaps even making their effects more powerful and intense.

What margin is there for thought, if it is gripped by fear at stepping into the outside – if what everywhere dominates is a diffuse exophobia? Where knowledges are handed over to calculation and to technologically assisted simulation; where procedures of simplification spread, peddled as truth-procedures; and where all understanding has its own place and performative function – then philosophy ends up being divested of its role. The sheer compactness of the saturated world demands a knowledge-regime which indulges it and remains within the prescribed limits.

If each ambit of knowledge is based on some problem, then philosophy poses a problem to the problems. It interrogates even the interrogator, knocking him out of his position, deposing him from his pulpit, and making him into the interrogated. The philosopher cannot escape this continual interrogation, which is, in a sense, a moment of splitting which takes the form of a question to the question.

Philosophy has forever been atopic; and in a world without an outside, it is dangerously out of place. A thinking-beyond, a vocation of the beyond, it seems unclassifiable, impossible to set within confines. Philosophy's territory is a paradoxical one, deterritorialised and inhabited by atopia. In its decentring movement, philosophy emigrates toward an outside from which it turns order upside down. To think estranges – makes foreign.

This book travels a path which follows the two trajectories of existence and politics, and whose time is patterned by three Greek words: *atopía*, *uchronía* and *anarchía*. If, in their close connection they preserve their alpha privative – the tension internal to philosophy – with their synergy they bring the critical impulse out into the open. They let its promised explosive charge to filter out into the beyond.

Thus, in touching on a theme subject to a prohibition – a verdict almost beyond appeal – this book summons philosophy back to its political vocation. This vocation is understood in terms of a reciprocal relation, where philosophy is not only inspired by the *pólis* but aspires to the *pólis*. It is, therefore, a political vocation because its inclination is to be found in the *pólis* itself. Thus, philosophy is summoned to make its return, without ever forgetting that it is out of place and out of step with the times – particularly in the city. After a long absence in which it has lost its voice, philosophy is called on, invited to draw the community back into the light, to reawaken it. For no community can do without an alert philosophy keeping watch.

Heraclitus said as much, and Plato backed this up in his great political dialogue, the *Republic*. It is not enough to think as in a 'dream', *ónar*, in a dreamlike condition. The thinking of whoever is alert, awake, in fact proves to be something quite different (see the *Republic*, 476c). The waking vision, *húpar*, is the very characteristic of philosophy, its distinctive trait, to the point of becoming its symbol. One can spend one's life asleep, or else awake and keeping watch. Those who do not philosophise doubtless do live. But their existence is diminished, their participation in politics compromised.

5

Wonder – a troubled passion

Philosophy is a Greek word. It is the product of a compound: *phileîn*, to desire, to have the ambition, to love; and *sophía*, which, even before meaning wisdom, indicates knowledge. First of all, *savoir faire*, practical abilities. Like those of artisans, of they who know how to build ships, to play musical instruments, to compose verse, but also the abilities of the legislator or politician. When democracy is making itself felt, multiple competences are needed to get by in the city. For instance, it is necessary to be able to speak well, to defend oneself, or to intervene in debates. Here a new figure crops up: the figure of he who not only possesses some knowledge but is also prepared to sell it. This is the *sophistés*, an expert in both private and public life, the master of rhetoric, who teaches for money and who – shading into a negative meaning of this term – turns out to be an impostor and charlatan.

Standing up against the sophists are those in the city who, precisely because they are considered expert and capable, risk being taken for sophists. Socrates was first among them. But there is a profound difference in their case: for they do not boast of having any knowledge which they do not. What inspires Socrates' questions is what he desires, not what he has. A desire for wisdom? Not exactly. It is difficult to believe that, as some suggest, the Greek word *sophía* is etymologically linked to *saphés*, which means clear, manifest. Yet Socrates not only does not claim to possess anything – least of all the truth; he moreover confesses that his burning ambition is to arrive at clarity. This knowledge of not knowing is the aporetic beginning of philosophy. Lovers of *sophía* – Plato repeatedly insists – are they who are driven by the desire to access knowledge, rather than be left obtuse and uncultured by ignorance.[1]

The terms 'philosopher' or 'philosophise' appeared here and there already before Socrates, following the frequently recurring model of compounds with the prefix *philo-*. For instance, they appeared in a fragment from Heraclitus (B 35), in Herodotus' histories (I, 30) as well as in the funeral oration that Thucydides has Pericles giving in memory of the soldiers who had fallen in the Peloponnesian war. 'For we also give ourselves to bravery, and yet with thrift; and to philosophy, and yet without mollification of the mind' (II, 40, 1).[2] The two verbs *philokaleîn* and *philosopheîn* are proudly proclaimed. Fifth-century BC Athens aspired to the beautiful and to the clear. This anticipates a *tópos* that will recur frequently throughout this text: for just as what is beautiful is not useful, the *sophía* to which philosophers aspire evades any criterion of usefulness.

If for Thucydides philosophy was a peculiar prerogative of the Greeks, for Plato and for Aristotle it distinguishes humanity itself. All aspire to that knowledge of knowledges, to that non-knowledge which can provide the only basis for wisdom. Plato specifies its origin: *thaumázein*.[3] To philosophise is, first of all, to look around oneself in wonderment, to interrogate, marvelled. More than an action, it is something one experiences. It is, therefore, a *páthos*, a passion whose hold one cannot escape. Whoever philosophises is ineluctably bewildered. And the inverse is also true: who does not feel bewildered cannot philosophise. The beginning is not a beginning, like when one sets some action going. For *páthos* is something one experiences: it comes from outside, is produced by another. What bursts into one's field of vision is surprising, extraordinary, it has no place in the ordinary; it leaves everything out of sorts. Yet the philosopher passively allows herself to be taken away by marvel at what she has around her, which strikes and disconcerts her, in a crescendo. She does not remain stubbornly impassive, coldly indifferent. On the contrary, she is aghast. For what previously seemed obvious to her no longer is. At a stroke, all her certainties melt away and everything wobbles. A certain malaise is inevitable, here. The *páthos* of philosophy is a passion. It consists of allowing oneself to be disoriented. It is wonder that drives the desire to know, but this wonder itself serves to debunk the knowledge that has been learned (see Aristotle, *Metaphysics*, 982b).

But is this not, at least in part, also the approach followed by those who study nature? Such an objection seems more than justified. Aristotle describes the procedure followed by the scientist who, once he has arrived at understanding, frees himself from wonderment. But if this also applied to philosophy, then philosophy would itself end as soon as that destination had been reached. This conception prevails among those who see philosophy as, at most, a duplicate of science. Moreover, for them it is a duplicate that becomes ever more useless as science makes progress. At root, even the scientist stands bewildered faced with whatever unknowns he runs into. But what grips him is not passion, but rather his curiosity. He does not yet understand, but readies himself to observe, to survey, to examine. The Greeks termed *theoría* that contemplation of things which accompanies wonder.

The philosopher and the scientist would seem to advance in tandem, brought together by a shared wonder, a shared theory. Both stumble across something which they find striking, and which they thus try to observe. But the similarity stops there. For the scientist, the surprising represents a problem that can be resolved through method, on the basis of already acquired results, with a view to a more extensive understanding of the object, its qualities, its substance. For the philosopher, too, wonder is connected to *theoría*. Surprised, she hones her sights. It is thus wonder that makes things visible. The philosopher – who is certainly not lacking in senses – opens her eyes. But philosophy demands that the eyes, having been opened, are then closed in order to allow for that singular way of seeing that is thought. Whoever philosophises closes her eyes and takes a step back in order to gather her thoughts, to avoid distraction. Yet philosophy is not characterised by this marvelled turn toward some thing. Rather, what characterises it is the conversion of a gaze directed toward some theme which is at the basis of the disconcertment. Thus, the philosopher remains faithful to her wonder – which is radical, just like the question she poses. This consternation runs through all the Platonic dialogues and culminates, so to speak, in the embarrassment of not even knowing *what is* this I who does not know. Philosophy springs precisely from this embarrassment, which shakes whoever philosophises.

Science follows a straight path – one which, leaving behind it the surprising, the strange and the disconcerting, proceeds toward the disenchantment of the world. One obstacle after another falls down, while the understanding grows. Such is the progress of science. Philosophy does not follow this course. Still less does it settle – as some would claim – for providing a justification for science's approach. Therefore, anyone who suggests that philosophy's task lies in an accumulation of understanding, in the endeavour to justify scientific concepts, methods and aims or to offer some 'ultimate foundation' for them, misses the target.

Philosophy does not come after science – it precedes it. It is already there, at the beginning. It has a much vaster dominion – a varied, blurry, jagged landscape of arduous ascents, of a series of turning points and switchbacks, where paths can suddenly break off. Even if she does make it to the top, whoever philosophises finds no satisfaction in the understanding she did not have before, in the solution to the problem. Rather, she is even more troubled and tormented, because from atop that promontory, which she imagined to be a lofty summit, she more clearly sees everything that is in the dark. And yet she continues on, troubled and perturbed. The philosopher's wonder is not naive. It is not satisfied by seeing some previously unknown thing which she finally seems able to grasp. Hers is an intensified wonder, almost another passion. Why is there something and not nothing?

Thus, the philosopher's path is anything but a straight line. On closer inspection, it is not even an outward journey, but a return home. Once the gaze has turned away from things which it leaves up to science, it curves, turns, folds in a different direction, to focus in on questions which are and will remain both ultimate and primary. This veering move can be called reflection, a change of course which reawakens from dreamlike sleep.

This path of return proceeds from the aporia of non-knowledge and heads toward clarity. But it never truly arrives at this destination, since whatever is sought hides and draws further away. It is on the philosopher's path that there comes into view the limit proper to human finitude, the limit of a mortal existence unable to tie the end to the beginning. Understanding the whole is precluded. How, then, can one not aspire to clarity, not desire it, love it? Hence why the Greek *phileîn* assumes such a decisive role in Plato, in indicating philosophy (see *Symposium*, 203b-204b). Love is a passion far more overwhelming than wonder, and it ends up supplanting it. Or rather, *sophía* itself is subordinated to *philía*. For what matters is the outburst of desire, the unstoppable restlessness, the misery, which together make philosophy into a vocation.

6

Between heavens and abysses

On a night when the face of the heavens seemed brighter than ever, an astronomer who ventured out to watch the stars each night ended up falling into a well. Such was the story as Aesop told it in one of his *Fables* (65). But there are also other versions of this anecdote. The most famous is that offered by Plato, who has Thales of Miletus instead of the astronomer.

The doxography has only scant knowledge of Thales. The founder of the Ionian school and a citizen of Miletus, 'after politics' – Diogenes Laërtius writes – he dedicated himself to the study of natural phenomena (I, 23-A1). He discovered new constellations, inspected the movements of the stars, calculated solstices and equinoxes; he must have been a talented geometrist, indeed, if he really managed to measure the height of a pyramid on the basis of the shadow it cast. He was perhaps the first to consider the soul immortal. Obscure – and controversial – is his connection with the hylozoistic doctrines that saw 'life', *zoé*, in all 'matter', *húle*. It seems that, when he observed a piece of amber or a magnet, Thales recognised a certain 'soul' even in what seemed to be inert. And he thus came to say that 'everything is full of gods' (B 22). His name is also attached to water *qua* first principle – indeed, he identified water as the source and the wellspring of all things.

But it was Plato who granted Thales everlasting fame thanks to the anecdote narrated in his *Theaetetus*. While Thales was 'watching the stars', *astronomoûnta*, and 'looking up high', *áno bléponta*, he 'fell in a well', *phréar*. Plato says nothing about the context for this incident. It is not known whether it happened in the middle of the countryside, if this learned man had ventured there, heedless, in order to contemplate these astral bodies in their regular orbits, or if it instead took place next to some orchard, already almost at the edges of the city, or even in some run-down street of Miletus itself. What is certain is that if Thales had stayed at home and studied the sky from his window, he would have avoided this pratfall. The origin of this inauspicious event lay in the fact that he left his home, went out – the horizontal movement punished, so to speak, by a vertical plunge. This punishment would stand as a warning for future philosophers who too unscrupulously dare to venture into a kinetics of external latitude. For there are wells, precipices and ravines lying in ambush.

The story has other surprises in store. The spotlight is snatched from the wise man by a woman, no less – chronologically, she appears as the second protagonist but she is, perhaps, the decisive one. She is the legendary 'Thracian slave girl', the spectator to this tragicomic tumble. Could anyone not share in her mirth? Even Plato seems to do so, as he comes close to taking sides with this 'neat, witty' young woman. Indeed, he writes that she makes fun of Thales, telling him that 'he was so eager to know the things in the sky that he could not see what was there before him at his very feet'.[1]

This clashes somewhat with the version provided by Diogenes Laërtius. He tells the story after underlining an ugly, distasteful aspect of Thales, who – according to this malign tradition – was thankful for his lot in life on three counts: 'to be a man and not a beast, male and not female,

Greek and not barbarian' (I, 34-A1). If this is what he thought of women, then it must be admitted that fate gave him his just deserts. As Thales groans in a ditch, he is reproached by 'an old woman' who had accompanied him; her words are similar to the young slave girl's, just the other way around: 'Do you, O Thales, who cannot see what is under your feet, think you shall understand what is in heaven?' From this version more clearly emerges the intention and resolution to observe – it is said that Thales went 'out of the house to study the stars'. Was it perhaps because of this eagerness, itself almost fussy and methodical, that he ended up falling? Or was it all unforeseeable? It is, after all, possible that as Thales went along his way he was suddenly enraptured by the beauty and the perfection of the cosmos at night, and thereby plunged into the hole. In short, it is uncertain if the object of scorn, here, is Thales' obstinate focus on his research – so absolute that it leads him to neglect the immediacy of what he has right in front of him – or precisely his capacity for wonderment, that enviable passion, so intense that it drags him along even at the risk to his own safety.

Hans Blumenberg reconstructed the immense success of this anecdote; it was destined to become the scene of the very dawn of philosophy, given the influence it had over its history.[2] Indeed, it was in many ways prophetic. The conflict between the philosopher and the city is prefigured within the latent tension. The mocking reproach, of which the 'slave girl' here becomes the spokeswoman, is the same one which common sense would incessantly level against the philosopher: that he claims to know that which is distant, but is unable to acknowledge that which is close at hand; that he looks up high and ends up plunging down into a pit. What use are stars if you do not even know how to walk down on earth? How can such an unbalanced and foolish type – anything but a sage or a wise man – have anything to teach to others?

Seized by wonderment, the philosopher sees what the others do not see and – vice versa – does not see what everyone sees. This striking distraction from the common sense would come at a hefty price; for the prosaic laugh would give way to much more hostile and violent forms. In a tragicomedy which passed also through farcical settings, dark, baleful, cruel tones came to prevail, leading up to the final drama. Scorn, ridicule and sarcasm would harshen to become accusation, reproach, condemnation. If the philosopher – that strange type who goes around watching the stars and falling into wells – had once already taken deserved punishment for his irritating lack of good sense, in the future the city itself would take care of punishing him. There are different ways of losing your head – by wonderment or on the scaffold.

The dynamic of conflict sharpened when the philosopher left the countryside, orchards and alleyways behind and arrived in the main square. Not least since his intention was not just to teach knowledge, but rather to show others that they simply *did not know*. The comedy before the well transformed into the tragedy before the tribunal, the half-innocent spectator into an assembly of legal hangmen, the unfortunate incident into execution for a capital crime. In brief: Plato turned the innocuous Aesopian fable into the pre-history of the drama lived by Socrates, by projecting the tension that cut through Athens onto this Ionian landscape. Already in this auroral scene, one can sense the effects that theory provokes.

Fascinated by the sublime aspect of the cosmos, Thales did not stumble. He could have put a foot wrong or tripped on a stone. But more simply, he plunged, fell down, to the bottom. The ground was no longer there for him and he experienced the void that opened up instead. This was a sort of *contrapasso* – but not so much for he who neglected the ground because he was watching the sky, as for those who imagine that thinking is just calm, peaceful contemplation, as persistent and regular as the orbiting of the stars, and presumed their own sovereignty over it.

But it is thought that comes and goes, through leaps and intuitions, that strikes like an unexpected idea, and likewise rapidly dissipates. In his account, Plato uses the verb *lantháno* to say that Thales did not realise, almost forgot, what he had under his feet. Thought is that which comes out of oblivion, that which endures. The reference is to the abyssal depth which only the philosopher hazards to survey, even if only fleetingly, for a second. Even if that means risking his own life. Perhaps for this reason, the concave space – the mirror of the convex face of the stars – would, in later versions of the anecdote, become a hole or a ditch, in order to avoid jeopardising the philosopher's very survival.

But it is impossible to identify all the countless meanings that skies and abysses would take on across philosophy's centuries-long history. We need only mention Kant's frozen 'starry firmament' covering the 'moral law', Heidegger's troubling *Abgrund*, the abyssal depths upon which existence stands. Surprising though it may seem, philosophers would feel more protected in this kinetics of verticality, up high or down low, according to an admirably variegated symbology. But a horizontal kinetics would prove much more adventurous and full of the unforeseen.

The gaze toward the sky betrays an aspiration which must have been widespread right from the outset: that of divining the future. Thales, too, was tempted by this, though at least it can be said that he was an expert in astronomy. According to the doxography, he managed to predict the solar eclipse in 585 BC (A 17). An indirect confirmation comes from another famous tale, this time narrated by Aristotle, in his *Politics*. Again, the theme is disdain toward theory, but this time it is vaunted not by a single Thracian slave girl but by the entire community of Miletus. For the first time, an explicit accusation was pronounced – one destined to have a far-reaching and protracted success.

Aristotle writes that 'since he was so poor', *dià tèn penían*, his fellow citizens damned Thales for the 'uselessness of philosophy', *hos anopheloûs tès philosophías*. But then, thanks to his astronomical calculations, he managed to foresee an abundant olive harvest; having a small amount of money available, he bought up the olive presses of not just Miletus but also Chios, even in the heart of winter when there was no demand. The 'time', the *kairós*, of the harvest arrived. Everyone was urgently looking for olive presses. Thales rented them out at a hefty price and earned a lot of money. So, the happenings in the sky served to orient him down on earth.

Such was the riposte from the philosopher who temporarily donned the vest of the wheeler-dealer, who abandoned his reflection and speculation to try his hand as . . . a speculator. And he succeeded, because he saw earlier and further than others. But his ambition was not monetary gain. Aristotle comments that Thales 'prov[ed] that it is easy for philosophers to be rich if they choose, but this is not what they care about'.[3] So here, after the surprise of the well, came Thales' redemption. Able to predict even what was supposedly unpredictable – phenomena both celestial and earthly, the eclipse of the sun and the olive harvest – he temporarily entered into the logic of the economy using his calculations, only to prove that this is not the logic proper to philosophy. This did not mean that the tension with his fellow citizens went away – indeed, it could only become sharper, if their values were so opposed. Even if philosophy really was 'useless', it was proving to be a subversive threat to the city.

7

Socrates' atopia

Extravagant, eccentric, extraordinary, strange – perhaps foreign? Doubtless surprising, incomprehensible, irritating. Socrates, a man out of place. The Greek epithet, which seems almost to have been coined for him personally, is *átopos*.[1]

But what does *atopía* mean? In the *Phaedrus*, the word indicates the disturbance produced by the unexpected and unusual. Other than being an affect of the soul, *atopía* is the characteristic of those who disconcert others. Thus, in the *Symposium*, when Alcibiades wants to relate Socrates' memorable feats, he ends up dwelling only on the singular, bizarre, eccentric ones. This then persisted in the recollections of both contemporaries and those who came after.[2]

Socrates is the philosopher's wonderment personified – the *thaûma* par excellence. He attracts and repels, fascinates and disturbs. The effect Socrates produces has been compared to a 'viper's sting', or else the electric shock from a 'flat torpedo sea fish' that 'benumbs whoever approaches and touches it'. Socrates defined himself as a 'horsefly' that bites.[3] Only a few would recover from those bites, from those blows, from those shocks. Most would be shaken under the impact of the trauma, and be left frustrated, embittered, offended.

Socrates is the archetypal philosopher. And that means that, from the outset, philosophy has had a great estranging effect. It isn't for everyone. It is not soothing, consoling, reassuring. For some, it is pointless diversion, a childish hobby, while for others it is a dangerous game that dulls the senses, inebriates, leads to ruin (see *Gorgias*, 484c-486a). It is not easy to learn from it. And what kind of teaching would it even provide? Unlike the sophists, Socrates said that he did not know. Nothing is communicated – a blow is struck, and that's all.

Socrates was out of place, *átopos*. With him, a new human type made its entrance onto the stage of history: the philosopher.[4] Socrates was destined to everlasting fame on account of his singular enigma, re-read and interpreted by a long series of philosophers, although he left no writings of his own. Yet Socrates had been anything but silent; rather, he began a new genre – dialogue. After his death, his disciples, who wanted to memorialise a Socrates so intent on interrogating his many interlocutors, tried to reproduce his irreproducible oral dialogues in written form. But only fragments of that Socratic literature are extant.[5] Yet, two sources have reached us almost intact: the works of Xenophon, and in particular the *Memorabilia*, and then the dialogues from Plato. This latter was a devoted friend, a loyal and assiduous follower, a faithful disciple even to the point of identifying himself with the master. It was Plato, a fine portraitist, who stylised the image of Socrates and who made him into this new human type, the philosopher. The Socrates known to world history is Plato's Socrates.[6]

Where does Socrates end and Plato begin? Is it possible to recognise with any certainty whether the words transcribed by Plato were the same ones uttered by Socrates? These questions have long tormented scholars, and they are doomed to remain unanswered. For the point is something else. Socrates is the first philosopher; philosophy began with him.

The disruptive confrontation, the open declaration of *non*-knowledge, the succession of question after question – what strange beginning is this? It is a knowledge that institutes itself on the basis of a non-knowledge. That is how philosophy began – or better, didn't begin. How is it possible to begin from a question that presupposes another, and which itself springs from non-knowledge? Philosophy does not proceed leaving some beginning behind it – though that would be a fine Ariadne's thread. More than that: it removes any beginning. Not in the Hegelian sense of overcoming, but in the sense that it fundamentally undermines any such beginning. Any *arché* is, therefore, an-arch-ic. That which, so to speak, begins with Socrates, does not fit within the order of an *arché*. It is, rather, an inner tension, a division *in actu* of philosophy. The two figures of Socrates-Plato, Plato-Socrates, bring this splitting – doubling – moment clearly into view.

That is why it would be too easy, too dismissive, to make Socrates into just a myth, or worse, a fiction. One ought instead recall the reversal that appears in the image which Derrida discusses in his book *La carte postale*, where a little Plato peeks over the shoulders of Socrates, who is doing the writing.[7] For philosophy, this splitting is the very possibility of survival. The question must remain within the heart of the response, and non-knowledge at the basis of knowledge. Philosophy is always hanging in the balance, besieged by loss, put to the test by the negation which it must time and again metabolise. Moreover, in Socrates' own mouth, philosophy presents itself as an antidote, a *phármakon*, both remedy and poison. The greatest danger – and it was glimpsed already back then – does not come from the outside (from sophists, pundits, reporters, etc.), but from philosophy itself. And this danger lies in philosophy's temptation to close itself off unilaterally, to shake off the encumbering atopia which inhabits it.

So, here he is, hurrying along the avenues which surround the gymnasium, sitting at the money-changers' tables, heading toward the market, in discussion with a renowned politician, stopping off again with a couple of smiths and shoemakers, and then tirelessly continuing onward. What on earth will this mania to ask questions ever achieve? It seems that he forgets anything else. In winter as in summer he goes around barefoot, almost as if to spite the cobblers, always wearing the same threadbare cape. Moreover, he has a habit of listing everything he does not need – for he maintains that not to need anything is divine, or something close to it. He is also bizarre in aspect: bulging eyes, a stubby nose, fat lips. He looks like a Silenus or a satyr – like Marsyas, the flautist who enchanted with his music, in spite of his physical appearance. With his haughty, fixed and concentrated gaze, Socrates, too, managed to bewitch people with his speech. It is as if the ancient ideal of the city fathers, the *kalogathía*, shattered in Socrates; perhaps he had something 'good' (*agathón*) about him, though he did not have anything 'fine' (*kalón*). Anyone who did not know that he came from an old Athens family would have been inclined to take him for a foreigner.

Some of his fellow citizens would run away when they saw him approaching at a distance – for whoever got trapped in discussion was lost. Others considered him a timewaster, lampooned him, scorned, derided and insulted him; some even raised a hand to him. Whatever had the Athenians done wrong to deserve such a nonsense-merchant? And such a pesky and pedantic one, at that? Rather than dedicate himself to the stonecutter's trade in his father's workshop, this madman went around polemicising over pointless questions, speciously flipping discussions around and turning words on their heads. Thus, between one trick and another he threw the most commonplace ideas into doubt – even the ones everyone agreed on – and blathered about sacred matters. He recognised no authority and even mocked the sovereign *démos*. After posing a long string of problems he did not resolve even one of them; rather, he had the condescension to say that he did not know. In truth, he was content just to show others that they did not know, and took near-delight in leaving them humiliated. And what kind of person would like to hear themselves being called ignorant – not least in the public square? Many were insulted and had more than their fill of his pointless, dangerous cavilling. Only a couple of idle youths, dazed by his drivel, went around with him on his forays through the city.

But Socrates' strangeness does not finish here. His ability to withstand hunger, exertion and cold is proverbial. During the siege of Potidea, in that frozen winter when other soldiers were no longer able to find sufficient cover, he walked barefoot on the ice, sparking irritation among his fellow militiamen.[8] And in that same military camp, a ridiculous and yet stupefying episode took place. Alcibiades recounted it with some admiration. For twenty-four hours, Socrates sank into a meditation that seemed like a sort of trance, an obsessive, open-eyed dream.

> Immersed in some problem at dawn, he stood in the same spot considering it; and when he found it a tough one, he would not give it up but stood there trying. The time drew on to midday, and the men began to notice him, and said to one another in wonder: 'Socrates has been standing there in a study ever since dawn!' The end of it was that in the evening some of the Ionians after they had supped – this time it was summer – brought out their mattresses and rugs and took their sleep in the cool; thus they waited to see if he would go on standing all night too. He stood till dawn came and the sun rose; then walked away, after offering a prayer to the Sun. (*Symposium*, 220c-d).

If Socrates' abrupt absences seemed surprising, his raptures of ecstasy appeared sublime. The story goes that as Socrates collected his thoughts, separating himself from the surrounding world, and deaf to any call, he immersed himself in an extended silence. And when he went quiet, other people must have found this at least as troubling as his dialogues. Again, it is Alcibiades who confesses to him: 'You seem to me far more extraordinary [*atopóteros*], Socrates, now that you have begun to speak, than before, when you followed me about in silence.'[9] Perhaps the most famous scene is the one that the *Symposium* begins with. As he was heading to the banquet together with Aristodemus, Socrates started walking more slowly and, ever more concentrated in his own thoughts, told Aristodemus to go on without him. When he reached the hosts' house, Aristodemus discovered that Socrates was no longer following behind him, and wondered where he had ended up. The servant sent to fetch him came back reporting that Socrates was immobile, in silence, in the porch of a neighbour's house. His friend commented: 'it is a habit he has. Occasionally he turns aside, anywhere at random, and there he stands' (*Symposium*, 175b).

Soothsayers, sorcerers, diviners, wise men, mathematicians, grammaticians, comedians, poets, sophists – the Athenians saw all sorts. But Socrates is unique, impossible to classify, indeed, *átopos*. Alcibiades put it bluntly: 'with the odd qualities of this person, both in himself and in his conversation, you would not come anywhere near finding a comparison if you searched either among men of our day or among those of the past' (*Symposium*, 221b). Thus one can recognise the emergence of a new, unprecedented figure: the philosopher.

Socrates' peculiar trait is his eccentricity. It is especially apparent in the practice of his thinking. Socrates is present, but it is as if he were not, as if he suddenly found himself to be distant, in a separate world, in a mysterious elsewhere. Almost as if he were in dialogue with a demon. What other explanation can there be for this prodigy? It is impossible to find any distinct location for this philosopher. He seems, on each occasion, to arrive from some non-place that no one can determine. From the depths of the skies or of the earth? Certainly, he is not to be found on the surface. Perhaps he is not really even in the city. He roams around the *agorá* but transcends its limits. He wants to pull his fellow citizens along with him, into that elsewhere. He lives with others, but does not live like others. He seems like he is stateless, an expatriate in the *patriá*. Each time he criss-crosses the *pólis* he does so as a foreigner, observing its life 'from above' with his estranging gaze. Distance is needed to be able to see what would otherwise be too close to see. His forays into the outside world, his wandering between the market and the court, are digressions and, likewise, transgressions. He deviates, diverges, dissents – openly so. He has no fear of stopping here or there to isolate himself, in order to think. He is well aware that this behaviour of his can seem ambiguous, extravagant. Abandoning himself to the solitude of thought in the public square – what a dangerous enterprise this was!

Socrates openly embraces this. His atopia is a hetero-topia,[10] not simply out-of-place, but also an allusion to another place. If Socrates remains in the city even while he pushes outside of it through his thought, that is because this elsewhere of thought provides the lever to decentre the order of the *pólis*, which is too closed, asphyxial, homologated. And in so doing, he shows that this is but one possible order. Hence why he thought alone, but also thought with others. Can dialogue change Athens's future?

8

A political death

A summer's day, just outside the city, along the course of
the Ilissus. The landscape could not be more enchanting:
the shade of the leafy trees, the perfume of the blossoming
flowers, the pleasant spring water, the soft grass, the light
breeze that accompanies the cicada chorus. It seems almost
like a holy site. Socrates, who never goes out of the city
limits, is deeply struck by this and thanks Phaedrus for
having led him here: 'you have guided the stranger most
excellently, dear Phaedrus'.[1] This latter responds 'You are
an amazing and most remarkable [*atopótatos*] person. For
you really do seem exactly like a stranger who is being
guided about and not like a native.' The extraneousness is
not limited to the confines of the countryside, but concerns
all of nature. Hence Socrates admits 'Forgive me, my dear
friend. You see, I am fond of learning. Now the country
places and the trees won't teach me anything, and the
people in the city do' (*Phaedrus*, 230d).

Indeed, Socrates was disappointed by his study of natural
phenomena, his calculations on the position of the earth
and the rotations of the sky, and rapidly abandoned them.
He feared that in imitating those who explored nature –

like them immediately directing his attentions to the world of things, purporting to grasp them with the five senses – he would have ended up entirely blinding his own *psuché*, his own soul.

Plato uses the metaphor of the 'second voyage' to highlight this epochal turning point in philosophy. This was the term which the Greeks used to refer to a ship which, for lack of wind, could be driven only by oars. Breaking with this metaphor, he described it as a matter of taking 'refuge in discourse', in *lógoi*.[2] But Plato's tone here is humorous, and this should not go unmentioned. He considers the 'second voyage' much superior to the first, i.e. to direct experience. If Socrates takes refuge in discourse, it is because he does not have the arrogant presumption to be able to see things with his own eyes alone, and he is therefore prepared to listen to what others have to say. He chooses the community of *lógoi*, the dialogue. More than an escape, it is philosophy's entrance into the world of the *pólis*, of the community of the city. With Socrates, philosophy interrogates human actions, poses for the first time the question of good, discovers its political vocation.

Yet that entrance is more dramatic than imagined, and the city is full of dangers lying in ambush. Socrates wants his questions to awaken others from the sleep of illusions – first and foremost, from the illusion of knowledge. But not all are open to such an unwelcome, bitter wake-up call. With his forays into the *agorá*, exercising the maieutic art of his mother – which he preferred to his father's trade – Socrates wants to spark the rebirth of his fellow citizens' souls, which would in turn imply a rebirth of the city. But things turn out rather differently.

In his *Apology*, Plato reconstructs the events and tells of what drove Socrates to this otherwise incomprehensible behaviour. He invokes the oracle of Delphi, a sanctuary dedicated to Apollo which must have been particularly dear to Socrates, even if just for the inscription carved into one of its walls, 'know thyself'. On one occasion his friend Chaerephon asked the oracle if there existed a man wiser than Socrates. The reply was that no one was wiser. What did these enigmatic words mean? What did the god mean? Socrates was truly amazed by this – for he knew that he did not know. To decipher its meaning, he was compelled to refute, *elencheîn*, the oracle and to question his own knowledge of not knowing. The philosopher's vocation is a provocative one – and it does not stop even before the words of the oracles.

So, Socrates went around the city interrogating his fellow citizens. First off, he turned to a well-known politician. Chatting with him, Socrates realised that neither of them knew anything good or fine; while the politician was convinced that he did know – but didn't – Socrates, conversely, neither knew nor believed that he did. His line of questioning among poets and artisans had the same outcome. In fact, in this latter case the results had, at first, seemed rather better. For they showed that they were experts in their own field. But immediately after that they made the same mistake, presumptuously holding forth on complex questions of which they knew nothing. All that was left for Socrates was to confirm what the oracle had said; its words were to be interpreted as if to say 'This one of you, O human beings, is wisest, who, like Socrates, recognizes that he is in truth of no account in respect to wisdom.'[3]

Such is the paradoxical definition of the *philo-sophos* in the Socratic-Platonic sense, in which the accent falls on the *ouk* – on the 'not', on negation. Philosophy's distinctive trait is *not*-knowing. This provokes difficulties and embarrassment – if only in the act of reformulation. Many interpreters would be tempted either to soften the negation, for instance speaking of a 'learned ignorance', or in any case put a positive spin on such an eccentric judgement. But non-knowledge is exactly what needs to be preserved, for it indicates something apparently simple which, on closer inspection, is in fact complex. Socrates does not understand anything, does not know any of the arts, does not master any trade. Yet, unlike others, he detects the limit, sees the impossibility of access. Thus, the mistaken transpositions do not escape him. One can and one must perfect knowledge, but without thereby laying claim to a divine knowledge. This person pointing out the limit – who evidently has a sharper eye, a further level of insight – is the philosopher.

What Socrates *knows* – that of which he is not ignorant – is his own non-knowledge. The Greek expression is *súnoida emautôi*, generally translated as 'conscious', 'conscious even of my own self' (*Apologia*, 21b, 22c-d).[4] The verb *su-neidénai*, from the preposition *sun-* ('with') and the verbal root *eid-oid* ('see'), would spread ever more often accompanied by the reflexive pronoun. Almost as if to underline the act of reflection. The literal translation would be 'I see with me within myself.' Thus also 'I am witness to myself.'[5] The Latin *conscientia* – and, from this, the English *conscience* – preserves very little of the complex semantics underlying this Greek expression, so important to philosophy. Socrates' knowledge does not have a substance, does not refer to some object. It is not even a knowledge, but rather a seeing within himself, a testimony of not knowing; to scrutinise oneself internally, *with* oneself, gives rise to a moment of splitting.

This way of seeing things – split, dual – has its concrete actualisation in dialogue, that *lógos* cut through by a *dia-*, 'by way of', 'between', a *lógos* divided by the distance produced by an opening. Plato would say that thinking is the soul's dialogue, *dialéghesthai*, with itself (*Theaetetus*, 189e). As for Socrates, the dialogues in the public square which played out under the sign of 'irony' – not taking oneself or others too seriously, that ingenuous dissemblance – lead only to *aporía*. Which means: a lack of a clear way forward, uncertainty, the impossibility of concluding, defining, of formulating a knowledge. Meno thus confesses: 'Socrates, I used to be told, before I began to meet you, that yours was just a case of being in doubt yourself and making others doubt also: and so now I find you are merely bewitching me with your spells and incantations, which have reduced me to utter perplexity.'[6] The verb *aporéo* indicates the hesitation of those who do not know how to proceed. This difficulty is, nonetheless, a beneficial one, for it is the sole condition for being able to both research and examine.

Here, one should not underestimate the political aspect, imagining that this search is somehow sterile. Socrates goes around interrogating people on what we would call questions of current affairs, themes that directly concerned the *pólis*. In the process of dialogue, he produces an estranging effect: he does not just disorient his interlocutor, but rather allows him to split in two, to separate himself from himself. Indeed, one part of his self would recognise himself in Socrates' words, being temporarily in agreement with him; thus, in this splitting moment, he in turn sees inside himself. Contrary to what is naively believed, Socrates' dialogue does not aim to achieve any kind of consensus. Rather, it seeks to spark discord even within the *psuché*, the soul of others, such that from there the discord may penetrate into and pervade the *pólis*. In this sense, Arendt is right to assert that Socrates made wonderment a public practice by introducing dual and dialogical thought into the city. It is, however, rather more difficult to believe that his ultimate end goal was the democratisation of democracy.[7]

Socrates' defeat is a certainty. This owed not to any supposed truth he was teaching, but rather to the dialogue that he everywhere brings with him – a great risk of discord in both the present and future life of the *pólis*. For this 'prophet' of thinking, who sought a city of justice, there was to be no way out, no path to safety.[8]

First came the ruinous war with Sparta, then the bloody oligarchic regime which would go down in history as the 'regime of the thirty tyrants', and finally a weak, culturally closed, politically small-minded democracy. The Athens of 399 BC was a city wracked by conflict and lacerated by resentment. It lived its irreversible twilight under the whip of a baleful mournfulness. This was the historical backdrop to an epochal trial which opened up the chasm between philosophy and politics. Socrates was tried *as a philosopher* whom the *pólis* could not and no longer wanted to host. And the fact that Socrates was an Athenian citizen – unlike others such as Anaxagoras or Protagoras, who had been exiled from the city – complicated the affair and heightened tensions to the extreme.[9]

The charge-sheet is passed down to us by Diogenes Laërtius: 'Meletus, son of Meletus of the deme Pitthus, has made the following charge against Socrates the son of Sophroniscus of the deme Alopeke: Socrates is guilty of not acknowledging the gods that the city acknowledges, but of introducing new divinities, and is guilty of corrupting the young. The penalty demanded is death' (II, 40). Those were certainly not novel accusations. For years, Socrates had been the target of calumnies, insults, derision. How could one forget Aristophanes' comedies?

Thus, when he mounts his defence, Socrates distinguishes between old accusers and new ones – and the former had been a much realer danger. The trial is itself tumultuous. Socrates speaks at length amidst Meletus' violent interruptions, fighting back point by point over the *asébeia*, the accusation of impiety, of having corrupted the youth, directed at the very man who had imagined a new education. Above all, he challenges the city. Yet this is not a unanimous verdict. Out of over 500 judges, there is only a thirty-vote margin. Thus, some aired the hypothesis of a light punishment, a monetary fine. Exile would be the solution. But Socrates does not give in. There is to be no deal, no agreement. Still less exile, given that he, an Athenian citizen, recognises the laws of the city. Rather, he asks to be kept alive on the Pritaneum, as a sign of gratitude for his contribution to the good of the *pólis*. Yet without doubt, as Merleau-Ponty wrote, he had 'a way of obeying which was a way of resisting'.[10]

Socrates' death is described in the *Phaedo*, the dialogue that Plato dedicated to the immortality of the soul. This text has had a very deep influence. The exemplary image of the dying philosopher has been a source of admiration and even of emulation. Above all, it inspired the conception of philosophy understood as practice for death. Here, we must at least cite the words of Cicero: 'the whole life of the philosopher ... is preparation for death', and of Montaigne: 'to philosophise is to learn to die'.[11]

It is not difficult to intuit that particular 'confidence with death' – as Rilke put it – that characterises the life of theory.[12] This is made clear in the *Phaedo* itself, where it is said that death is 'the release and separation of the soul from the body'. The task of philosophers lies precisely in the ceaseless attempt to untie and separate the soul from the body. They fear death less than others do, since for their whole lives 'the true philosophers practice dying'.[13]

Yet it is true that, over the centuries, fear has come to prevail. Philosophy has been driven to translate death into a form of immortality, or else to banish it completely. Thus, in his *Being and Time* Heidegger found an easy target when he accused Western metaphysics of having banished death.[14]

Many commentators, starting with Moses Mendelssohn, have emphasised the insufficiency of the three proofs the *Phaedo* employs to demonstrate the immortality of the soul. Orphean-Pythagorean myths remain lurking in the background, as attested by the ancient etymology *sôma-sêma*, suggesting a body which is a tomb for the soul; death will be nothing but a liberation from the earthly prison. But even Simmias and Cebes, the two Pythagoreans in dialogue with Socrates, no longer seem to believe this. Disenchantment now undermined the ancient tradition. For Cebes, the fate of the soul beyond the earth no longer meant anything, while Simmias laughed when Socrates said that to philosophise is to learn to die. For both, the soul is destined simply to dissolve. So, what use are these proofs? Did Plato perhaps not see how unconvincing they were? The answer comes in the concluding scene.[15]

The philosopher's final acts in his cell are described evocatively. The sun is now setting. His pupils around him break into tears. Socrates, however, calmly continues the dialogue, comforts the others, and maintains his composure as he drinks the hemlock. When almost all parts of his body are already cold, he exclaims: 'Crito, we owe a cock to Asclepius. Pay it and do not neglect it' (*Phaedo*, 118a). These are his final words.

But what does this mean? The Greeks sacrificed a cockerel to Asclepius, the god of medicine, as a sign of gratitude, when they were cured of some illness. So, what did Socrates want to say here? Why on earth make such an offering, if he was about to die?

Nietzsche shed light on this question better than anyone else. He insists that Socrates' last words ought not be taken lightly – they are not some innocuous piece of irony. In his *The Gay Science* he writes:

> Whether it was death or the poison or piety or malice – something loosened his tongue at that moment and he said: 'O Crito, I owe Asclepius a rooster.' This ridiculous and terrible 'last word' means for those who have ears: 'O Crito, *life is a disease.*' Is it possible that a man like him, who had lived cheerfully and like a soldier in the sight of everyone, should have been a pessimist? He had merely kept a cheerful mien while concealing all his life long his ultimate judgment, his inmost feeling. Socrates, Socrates *suffered life*! And then he still revenged himself – with this veiled, gruesome, pious, and blasphemous saying. Did a Socrates need such revenge? Did his overrich virtue lack an ounce of magnanimity? Alas, my friends, we must overcome even the Greeks![16]

When he invokes a well-known rite of thanks in the moment of his departure – at one step away from death – Socrates declares his gratitude, because he has been cured of the disease that is life itself. The philosopher's death is the confirmation of his life. In the time granted him on earth, he never relented from learning to die. Having migrated with thought, he now prepared for the final migration.

But in this scene – philosophy's most dramatic, and most

decisive – Socrates is also in dialogue with his friends and pupils surrounding him, who are destined to outlive him. He entrusts his words, his memory, to them. They continue to dialogue, adopting what he said as their own and proceeding with his teaching. This is immortality.

In his comments, Nietzsche speaks of revenge – a term loaded with meaning in his reflection, for it relates back to the 'spirit of Christianity'. Perhaps in this context, such a claim is excessive, hyperbolic; yet he makes well understood what he means. Plato transforms that death, makes it immortal, turns the defeat into a victory. Above all, it is a victory over the decadent city, but also a victory over the world. Veering away from the catastrophe of the *bíos politikós*, philosophy will erect another order, an extrapolitical city of memory. The life of theory distances itself from the *pólis*, its collapse now sealed by the infamous sentence passed against Socrates. Refusing to flee, he remains an Athenian citizen to the last. But in the moment of his death he becomes a witness to the post-political world, he stands up as a torchbearer for philosophy. Already strangers to the city, philosophers become foreigners everywhere in the world. Nor would they ever be able to forget the death of Socrates. In their exile, this appalling scandal would serve as the constant warning of a latent conflict with the city, one that had temporarily calmed but only been pitched into the future.

9

Plato – when philosophy headed into exile within the city

Socrates' execution represented a definitive caesura: it put an end to philosophy's fleeting and conflict-strewn idyll in the *pólis*. Nothing would be the same as before. For philosophers, life in the city had now become too dangerous. That was why many – in particular those who founded the various 'minor Socratic schools' – chose the path of exile. Was there, perhaps, some alternative? If Athens had condemned its most just citizen, the best man, a philosopher like Socrates, what could his pupils have expected?

At first, Plato also joined this exile. He left Athens for the shores of Syracuse in a first tumultuous voyage, marked by many misadventures. He returned from Sicily around 387 BC (see the *Seventh Letter*). He then acquired a piece of land near the little wood dedicated to the hero Academus, to the north-west of Athens's city walls, and founded a new school there. It should be presumed that a model philosophical commune which he had encountered during his visit to *Magna Graecia* contributed to the foundation of this school. Near Crotone there lived a group of semi-hermitical philosophers who, following in the footsteps of their master Pythagoras (who had passed away more than a century earlier) led a life of vegetarianism and dedication to the study of mathematics. Although they were separated from the city, they continued to reflect on political questions, as they had in the past. Plato detected, in this, a path that could also be followed in Athens.

What needed to be preserved, here, was the master's atopia. No more disdain, no more derision – no more death. Philosophical thought, that misunderstood ecstasy, must not be expounded in the public square. Adequate protection was needed against any potential violence. But it was not even remotely conceivable that the philosophers could abandon the city entirely, dooming them to hermitage. What was at stake, here, was the *bíos theoretikós*, their life of theorising, a life which was itself born within the city. What would have become of it on the outside, in an apolitical context? Perhaps it was possible to imagine retreating within oneself. This would have been a refuge for ideas, a shelter for philosophers and their absences, an abode where they could reflect, at due distance, on the good of the *pólis*. This would have allowed them to concentrate, and eased the philosophical flights 'into the depths of the earth' and 'above the sky', so well described by Pindar (see *Theaetetus*, 174a). There was, therefore, to be no new Atlantis, no utopia. Rather, the elsewhere of thought could be saved by translating atopia into a heterotopia – as per the Socratic ideal – and instituting it in a real place, close to the city, a school. Thus, another space based on its own laws – contrasting with and in some aspects opposed to the city's own – was opened up in the area of the *pólis*, a space where thought would be sovereign. This was Plato's great intuition when he founded the Athenian Academy. The philosophical elsewhere was redeemed and protected thanks to a heterotopic institution – one which would have decisive, enduring effects on world history. From Plato's *genius loci* – which inscribed the academy's difference on the architecture of the city – would spring forth all the 'sites' dedicated to the practice of thought: academies, universities, schools, monasteries, etc.[1]

Though defeated, the philosophers did not bend down to exile. Following Socrates' teaching, they returned – but they brought their exile back within the *pólis*. Their presence-absence would, in future, represent the stigma which Athens, deceitful and shameful, had so richly deserved. For now, philosophy's subversive activity was institutionalised in the Academy. What a humiliation for the *pólis* this was! For roaming around within its walls were these strange, eccentric individuals who lived in the city as if they were elsewhere, who resided there as foreigners. Indeed, they openly laid claim to this, paraded the fact. They were witnesses to another, better city, citizens of the *Allopolis* now established within the *pólis*.

In the garden of the Academy – neither *agorá* nor courthouse nor market – the philosophers could exercise themselves in observing the city from above, free to migrate in the skies of ideas. Who knew if the theorising-in-exile of these supra-citizens would ultimately prove harmful to public co-existence? The answer was especially in doubt given that, although they did not take part in the tumult, the hostilities, the mobilisation of the *pólis*, they did not seem to have stopped counting on supra-political fields.

Certainly, their lack of success, their loss, had left them with a certain melancholia, the indelible marker of Saturn. They would bear its trace for centuries, almost as a reminder of the epochal rupture with the city. It was meagre satisfaction to acknowledge that democracy had itself failed. The city was collapsing. This meant the end not only of the civilisation based on the *pólis*, but also of politics understood as a shared participation in the common good.

Born of Socrates' death, philosophy was thus the daughter of political defeat. But the Acropolis of thought managed to resist, for centuries and millennia. Thus, *philosophía* turned out to be the name for the capacity for exile. And philosophers, these saturnine witnesses, these transcendent inhabitants who had opted for permanent migration, knew how to convert this irreparable defeat into a future conquest.

10

Migrants of thought

It thus proved possible to overcome the political trauma, temporarily at least. But this could be done only by foreigners, and only by remaining in the city. This was how it would be possible to stay faithful to Socrates: by following in his footsteps. But the atopia grew, became exasperated, since it was no longer admitted in the *agorá*. Those citizens who, incapable of fully living the whirlwind of the *pólis*, began to take their distance from it – observing themselves in their own role with an eccentric gaze, as if from the outside – were driven into a logical exile. Thus, they became spectators of themselves and, at the same time, witnesses to the injustice to which the city had doomed itself. This gaze of theirs gave them the feeling of being a little outside and a little above – and certainly, like strangers. They were still citizens, but already they were no longer citizens. Moreover, the city considered the observers within its walls with some suspicion, taking them for potential enemies. Expatriates in their own *patriá*, these city-less types ended up declaring themselves 'cosmopolitans'. This term does not mean 'citizens of the world'. Rather, its meaning is both much graver and much more promising

– for it designates them as citizens of the cosmos, the subversive inhabitants of a future order.[1]

These non-citizens are philosophers. Their singular secession from the sphere of the real to the sphere of the possible, or better, of the impossible, which transfigures political defeat into philosophical privilege, sparks off the emigration toward theory. This is the debut, dejected yet magnificent, of the *bíos theoretikós*.

Many figures have explicitly recognised the extraneousness which permeates and underpins *theoría*; it is a recurring theme from Aristotle to Heidegger. In his *Politics*, Aristotle speaks of the philosopher who, far from actively participating in the *pólis*, withdraws to dedicate himself to thought alone. In this vein he speaks of *bíos xenikós*, a self-estranging life, the life of the foreigner (*Politics*, 1324a 16). If common sense sets one in harmony with a world in which one could feel comfortably at home, thought instead provokes disorientation, a sense of being out-of-place. Heidegger adopts an aphorism from Novalis: 'philosophy is really nostalgia, a desire to be at home everywhere'.[2] Yet, he warns that this is not a *Bestimmung*, a determination; it would be rather paradoxical to identify philosophy with nostalgia. Rather, taking due caution, one can say that homesickness, *Heimweh*, is the *Grundstimmung*, the disposition, the inclination, rather, the 'fundamental attunement' of philosophy.[3] The aphorism thus needs to be slightly amended, retouched. For one may feel a passing homesickness [*nostalgia*], insofar as one is no longer at home anywhere. Is this not the meaning of the rapture produced by wonder? Whoever is at one with the place they inhabit is satisfied in that seeming, immediate comfort – and denies themselves to philosophy.

Here, one cannot but make reference to Plato and his famous myth of the winged chariot. It would be impossible to understand the emigration toward the *bíos theoretikós* without recounting the fascinating metaphysical journey that precedes and prepares it. Life on earth is, perhaps, an exile, and *theoría* a route home.

Plato describes the lot of the human soul, whose symbol is a carriage driven by a charioteer – the symbol of reason – and pulled by two horses, one the image of generous desires and affects, the other of selfish instincts and impulses. It is these chargers who are making the chariot move, but it is the charioteer's job to hold the reins and stop the horses from clashing into each other. Just as the stars rise up in the night sky, thus human souls proceed on winged chariots toward the heights of the face of the cosmos. They follow the chariots of the gods who each day effortlessly carry off this same ascent. Having reached these heights, immortal souls pass outside; having taken a stand on the outer face of heaven, they soar, transported by its slow orbit which marks out regular revolutions and patterns the cycles of the cosmic year. As their gaze opens up to that infinite beyond, outside the world's own confines, they 'contemplate', *theoroûsi*, 'the things outside of the heavens', *tà éxo toû ouranoû* (*Phaedrus*, 247c).

In Greek, the word *ouranós* means 'covering' and suggests the face of heaven which covers the visible; truth is, therefore, that which is uncovered, unveiled. This place-beyond which no poet will ever be able to sing – the abode of thought where the intellect can observe the perennial form of being and immutable ideas like justice or temperance – is called *huperouraniós*, hyperuranius, supra-sky. Some see more, others less, some nothing at all. Unable to rise up, they are pulled along and submerged in the whirlwind. They clash together, are crowded together, trample on one another, in a terrifying disorder which leaves many of them mangled. The wings break. Thus, they drift away without managing to uncover the 'plain of truth', of *alétheia*, the meadow where the best food for the soul is cultivated, and thanks to which the wings can fly. Their fate is sealed by the law of Adrasteia, the law of the 'inevitable'. Weighed down by oblivion, they crash to the ground. In that exile, these souls seem condemned to wander through the millennia. The exceptions are the souls of philosophers – the only ones who do put on wings.

Remembering that vision, however imperfect, they try to return to the plain of truth, distancing themselves from the ins and outs of human affairs. The majority thus accuse the philosophers of being out of their minds.[4]

With this great myth, the central cornerstone of his metaphysics, Plato indicates the manner in which philosophy moves between land and sky. They who are at one with the place they inhabit remain wingless, unable to raise themselves up, full of themselves, their gaze folded downwards. For them, there is nothing but the brutality of life in exile. But nor do the gods philosophise, for they can take up a stand on the outer face of the cosmos and contemplate truth (see the *Symposium*, 204a). What is, instead, winged – and this alone – is the thought of philosophers. Interrupting the human exile, they temporarily depart from the pedestrian flatness; raising themselves up above, they inhabit an elsewhere, in a return journey, a subversive ascent. This turns them into uranic witnesses, able to watch the world down below – the world of the city – with hyperuranic eyes. Philosophers are the sublime migrants of thought. What would the city be without these supracitizens, these transcendent inhabitants, able to observe the *pólis* from up on high?

Hannah Arendt delved into the 'elsewhere' of thought in a chapter of her book *The Life of the Mind* bearing the almost provocative title 'Where Are We When We Think?'[5] She uses the example of Socrates' famous absences, sunk into himself, deaf to any outside appeal, isolated and absent. Arendt concludes that thought is not located anywhere. The place of the thinking I is a 'nowhere'.[6] It could be added that thinking subtracts itself from everyday topology and the principles of physics. Any attempt to localise in some part of the brain the thoughts a philosopher has in her study or in a lecture theatre will, then, prove to be entirely in vain. It was Wittgenstein who did most to deconstruct any traditional preconceptions regarding the spatial-temporal arrangement of thought, through the grammar of the verb *Denken*.[7] It is impossible to indicate any beginning, any end, any 'where'. At most, one can perhaps speak of an elsewhere, as opposed to a vaguer non-place.

Indeed, what can be taken for certain is that those who think will withdraw, as if into another world. Hence the impression of distancing, of absence, perceived also by many philosophers who – from Descartes to Merleau-Ponty – have related that estranging experience of solitude, which for others is strangeness. This would not be so if the condition of those who think were any normal condition of idleness. Rather, this is clearly something quite different: an engagement that takes over, absorbs and engulfs. As if those who think were called by distant voices in an indefinite elsewhere, who have set them off on that inner journey. And what is no less certain – as Arendt writes, citing Aristotle's *Protrepticus* – is that philosophers love this singular abode of their thought, as if it were their native place.[8]

Even if those who think seem to distance themselves from the world, their thought remains worldly. This explains why these subversive inhabitants' desertion of the city, their emigration into the sphere of the possible and the impossible, is not the prelude to an apolitical thought. Those who think are still in and of the world – in certain regards, even more so than others are. This *outside* stance, also in the particular sense Plato attributes to *éxo* in his myth, indicates the ecstatic aspect of thought which stretches out beyond, in the tension of the hyperuranic gaze. This ecstasy, which ought not in any way to be confused with phenomena of stupefaction, is intimately linked to existence. This does not only owe to the etymological connection repeatedly emphasised by Heidegger – *ékstasis* and *existentia*. For just as existence emerges in its thrownness, transcending itself in an ever-finite beyond, thus thought is a further, intensified coming-outside. Verticality is constitutive of existence. This apparent state of death is a more alive existence, one enriched by the excess of an elsewhere. Whoever immerses themselves in thought raises themselves up. In that sublime migration lies the existential impetus. Those who do not practise *theoresis* do not lead a life dedicated to the practice of thought; rather, they remain real, all too real.

Inscribed within existence itself, the impulse to distance oneself from the current of life in order to watch the theatre of the world from the outside has always manifested itself, albeit in different forms and modalities. Yet, only in the Greece traumatised by the death of Socrates were the – perhaps unique – conditions created for the *bíos theoretikós* to be defended, upheld, institutionalised by Plato, thus giving rise to philosophy and its history. The theoretical ascesis which Husserl, delving into the Greek archive, called *epoché* – that 'suspension, exercise in withdrawal, gathering' – marked the arrival on the scene of a new figure, that of the observer. This 'secession' is a capacity of exile, which ought not be confused with flight.[9] For, on the contrary, it carries a subversive potential. The contemplative life flares up when this politics has ceased to be a democratic passion. And in that already post-political horizon, after the defeat, the philosophers remain to recall the beyond of another world, from which they each time make their return to the city as asylum-seekers.

11

'What is philosophy?'

It is no exaggeration to say that philosophy is mired in a continual crisis of legitimacy, as if it were always being called on to justify itself. From the outset, multiple forms of defence have made up part of its history. On closer inspection, this is the backlash of the effects it provokes, from disorientation to critique. The anecdote regarding Thales shows as much. Other better-known apologias would follow. But the question of its *télos*, its purpose, had already been raised. Aristotle answered it only partially by observing that the philosopher could have become like the others if he wanted.

One can thus see why this kind of question follows philosophy around like a shadow. Such questions recur even where no shoots of polemic emerge; they are, in this case, attempts at normalisation. They nonetheless become more pressing when it is philosophy itself that loses sight of its vocation, entering into crisis or becoming ossified in a scholastic dogmatism.

'What's the point?' 'What good is it?' 'What is its purpose?' Even to reply is already to embrace a deceitful challenge, by accepting the presuppositions implicit within the question: that philosophy is a means useful to some end, an acting able to satisfy some expectation. With this externally imposed teleology, something is taken for granted which cannot be – namely, that philosophy is a means to an end, with some ultimate practical purpose. Thus philosophy, which stands apart from the economy of advantage and disadvantage, which is neither subordinate nor supraordinate, falling outside of any hierarchy, is forced to defend itself. Here lies the tacit further question: why bother, if it isn't useful for anything? These questions seek to put into doubt philosophy's very existence, reducing it to a surrogate that conforms to pre-established purposes and principles. They are, therefore, the hint of a dogged anti-philosophical prejudice.[1]

The fateful question 'what is philosophy?' ought to be taken in this same sense. Already just because it imposes a definition, or claims that philosophy ought to define itself. That the answers are not simple – just as in the case of other disciplines, from biology to physics – is obvious even from its name. Indeed, it is not called *sopho-logy*, i.e. the doctrine of knowledge, but *philo-sophy*. To conceptually define a *love for* something seems like an impossible endeavour. For love is always personal. And this also goes for philosophy, which if it loses this stamp becomes a mere academic exercise.

Posed again even in recent times, the question 'what is philosophy?' proves deceptive – lending itself to more than one misunderstanding. First of all, because it is impossible to understand whether this question centres on the word itself. Is the point to understand its meaning? To know what it designates? To know its usage or, as Wittgenstein would say, its 'grammar' – asking what phrases it recurs in? Or is it asking for a historical-conceptual reconstruction of the term and its many slippages, from Plato to Husserl? More often, the question is understood as a query posed to the single interlocutor – the philosopher him- or herself – with the effect that they feel they have the right to provide their own definition. As can easily be imagined, there are countless variants, not only on account of different tendencies or positions, but also because of individual perspectives. An individual definition would, then, purport to make universal claims, without considering the impossibility of finding any consensus. Even famous and widely shared definitions, like Hegel's – philosophy is 'its own time comprehended in thoughts'[2] – are no exception. For they, too, have been critiqued and openly challenged. It should be added that, in its presumption to 'classic' status, this question risks making philosophy eternal when, on the contrary, it is something that unfolds over time.

Heidegger's essay *What is That – Philosophy?* may have had a reassuring effect. If the most obsessively cautious philosopher, himself resistant to any definition, ventured such an endeavour, then his attempt must have constituted an important precedent. Usually these pages – the basis of a lecture given in Cerisy-la-Salle in August 1955 – are collated together with the more famous preliminary essay *What Is Metaphysics?* dating back to 1929. But here, on the eve of his *Being and Time*, Heidegger offered a striking synthesis of his critique of metaphysics, whereas in the subsequent text he turned from one question to the other in the most rapid of sequences. Even the titles (in German) were different: one is *Was ist Metaphysik?* and the other *Was ist das – die Philosophie?* Certainly, this was no accident.

Upon a closer reading of *What is That – Philosophy?*, it becomes clear that it does not in fact arrive at any definition. Whoever looks for one will be left empty-handed. From the first page to the last, Heidegger does nothing but put the question itself – and its legitimacy – into doubt. This becomes clear already when he denounces the danger of speaking 'about' philosophy, taking up a position above or outside of it, and thus points an accusing finger against any metaphilosophy.[3] It is better to cautiously venture into it rather than circle around it – it is better to philosophise. And this warning remains in place as he proceeds onward. In order to avoid losing his thread and falling into the purely arbitrary, Heidegger proposes a return to examine the word itself. Philosophy 'speaks Greek': it emerged in a European and Western historical tradition. Europe is intimately philosophical in origin. It would, then, be impossible to reply to the question 'what is philosophy?' except in dialogue with the thinking of the Hellenic world. But the question itself is Greek in its very formulation – for it translates the *tì ésti* introduced by Socrates in the Platonic dialogues. 'What is it?' – the accent falls on the *tí*, on the *qui*, on the *das*, on the 'what?' The question is destined to 'remain equivocal'[4] for one cannot tell whether it is asking about the meaning of the word – 'what it means' to speak of beauty, nature, good, etc., according to the Socratic modality – or if attention is focused on the *quidditas* of the scholastics, on essence. If that were true, then it would be a matter of defining the essence of philosophy.

Heidegger not only carefully avoids answering, but defends his choice of the title *Was ist das – die Philosophie?* The provocation, here, is that *das* breaks up the classical formula, interrupting it, thus inviting reflection on the meaning of this question. 'What is that – philosophy?' It is impossible to define the essence of philosophy. Whether because one would fall into the metaphilosophical snare of imagining oneself above philosophy, or because the question is not gnoseological – it does not lead to any knowledge. Nor is it historiographical, and thus even tracing philosophy's development does not itself exhaust the question.

On closer inspection, whoever asks what philosophy is knows already. The question springs from philosophy itself. With a hermeneutical circle, Heidegger shows that the question mark – betraying the wish to break out of that circle – is artificial. It is raised only when the relationship with philosophy becomes problematic, confused, obscure. It is pointless, then, to place one's trust in empty affirmations or simply seek the answer in a philosopher, for instance in Aristotle: 'It is one thing to establish and to describe the opinions of philosophers. It is an entirely different thing to talk through with them what they are saying, and that means, that of which they are telling.'[5]

Heidegger does not define the essence of philosophy; indeed, with his obsessive questioning, he makes it possible to detect the risks of any such definition. This attitude is consistent both with what he had earlier defended and what he later went on to write. In short, what is at stake for Heidegger is to rethink philosophy after the end of philosophy. This is what he asserts in an essay dating from 1964 and published a few years later, *Das Ende der Philosophie und die Aufgabe des Denkens*.[6] For Heidegger, it is necessary to acknowledge two concomitant phenomena: on the one hand, the ending of a historical cycle, the cycle of metaphysics, which runs from Plato to Nietzsche; on the other, the definitive separation of scientific knowledges, also thanks to technology. What are the implications for philosophy? Can it do anything except fall into line, in uniformity with metaphysics or technology? In German, *Ende*, end, is synonymous with *Ort*, place, and Heidegger – referring precisely to this meaning – indicates that philosophy, having become something else, must rethink itself starting from this extreme place; not exhaust itself or finish, but rather, dislocate itself, which then also means to rethink itself.

Philosophy does not come and go, does not finish. Kant speaks of a 'natural disposition' of the human being.[7] Everyone philosophises – sometimes without being aware of it. Even children are already asking themselves about the future, death, happiness. Philosophy is not a discipline (even if it is, in part, institutionalised), it is not a specialist knowledge, or a craft or an occupation. It wanders here and there, also into the public square, in diverse forms, often changing its guises; at times it seems to be philosophy and is not, at other times it does not seem to be so but is – and philosophers recognise it. One could simply say that 'philosophy is philosophizing'.[8] Only some have the particular destiny of awakening others to philosophy – yet, far from being the privilege of a few, it is existential, in the sense that it touches on the very foundation of existence. Heidegger writes: 'Philosophizing itself is rather a fundamental way of Da-sein. It is philosophy which, in a concealed way for the most part, lets Da-sein first become what it can be.'[9] Thus intimately human, so ineluctably mortal, philosophy maintains itself, as the name suggests – this love for... this nostalgia over... – in the horizon of finitude. And it's known already that the gods don't philosophise.

12

Radical questions

What distinguishes philosophy is the question. Precisely because it does not have a determinate object or method or end, its fleeting and paradoxical *ubi consistam* lies in interrogating itself. An interrogation which always-already indicates the escape route beyond any possible response.

There are no phenomena, laws of nature or social customs which can evade philosophy's inexorable, obstinate interrogation. Nothing can elude it – even nothing itself. 'Why is there something rather than nothing?' Formulated by Leibniz, this is the exemplary question of philosophy. What others consider obvious, striking, taken for granted, in the philosopher's eyes loses any aura of solemn and sure gravity that would protect it from questioning. Everything is exposed to interrogation; nothing can be imposed, or indeed presupposed, beyond doubt.

But here lies the significant difference with science, since all science elaborates its demonstrations on the basis of principles, fundamental concepts, first propositions, which it is nonetheless unable to demonstrate by scientific means. Plato clarifies this well when he focuses on the approach taken by mathematicians and geometrists concerned with calculations or figures. They set out from a 'hypothesis' and from there move toward a conclusion, without ever returning to the principle, of which they do 'not deign to render any further account ... to themselves or others' (*Republic*, 510c). Indeed, the Greek word *hupó-thesis* – akin to *hupotíthemi*, place under – means 'supposition, premise'. That goes for the triangle, for the diagonal, for geometric figures, but also for numbers, odds and evens.

In the scientific approach, the hypothesis takes up the place of a principle and foundation, becomes *arché*. It is here that the philosopher intervenes, to return to that starting point, to that presupposition that cannot be taken for granted. She takes a step back in order to annul, to abdicate, that principle, interrogating it, showing that the principle is only *hypothetically* a principle. She thus arrives at *anhupótheton* – that which is without presuppositions. With her questioning she goes beyond any hypothesis, surpasses the limitations of individual scientific disciplines, transcends the limit. She takes what is beyond question for science and raises it to the dignity of philosophical questioning.

In an analogous fashion, Kant issues a call not to confuse philosophy with mathematics, even though it, too, is also a conceptual construct. But philosophy, even in just interrogating the status of mathematics, already transgresses and transcends its limits. Philosophy is, therefore, 'transcendental philosophy'. One should recognise, with Kant, the metaphysical value of the philosophical question, which goes beyond that which is presupposed in the sciences, exceeds the positivity of knowledge, the self-evidence of principles.[1] Decisive, here, is the limit. The sciences are circumscribed in a dual sense: they cover only some field of knowledge and they do not know their own presuppositions. On the contrary, philosophy's job is, in each case, to show the limit. Thus proceeding without back-up, passing beyond the lines, breaking through the borders, philosophy safeguards openness, protects the open.

The questions posed by philosophy are, therefore, limit-questions, posed from the limit, precisely in order to climb over it. It is in this sense that philosophy does not come after the sciences, but rather precedes them; it is not subsequent and successive but originary. Its questions are fundamental in the sense that they go to the foundation, get to the principle, in order to interrogate it, shake it around, uproot it. Philosophy's question is not a matter of interrogating just anything. It is a radical question. For it gets to the roots. It does not ask in order to know. It scrutinises not knowledge in general, but rather the ultimate foundation of the possibility of knowledge, in order to put it into question. One could thus say that philosophy is a theory of ultimate things. It is thus contiguous to eschatology. Except that in its extreme radicality, philosophy makes no exception even for discourse on the *éschaton*, on the ultimate limit. And it subjects its own interrogation to the most radical questioning. Whoever philosophises does not ask in order to know. For instance, what time is. What gives rise to philosophy is the gnawing concern of not knowing what the word 'time' means. Whatever is known becomes worthy of questioning, and knowledge – revealing itself to be non-knowledge – is exposed to a questioning which must incessantly re-emerge. Where there is no longer questioning, there is no philosophy.

To claim some solution would be like demanding that philosophy wind itself up. Philosophy does not resolve problems. Deriving from military verbiage, the *próblema* – from *probállo* – is that which protrudes, a promontory, but also a shelter and a bulwark, the obstacle that presents itself, the difficulty. It is the query that demands a response, the enigma that needs unravelling, and it has its paradigm in the mathematical problem. In short: problems are resolvable assignments. Once the solution is found, the obstacle is overcome and the problem disappears. Which is not to say that further problems may not then arise. One can speak of definitive solutions only in mathematics: outside of that field, one finds solutions which, if not truly unambiguous, do at least appear to be the optimal ones. Philosophy is not in the business of providing definitive solutions. Otherwise philosophy would not have a history in which the questions that assail it – on truth, on good, on liberty – are always proposed anew, in ever-different forms. The basic problems of philosophy are, rather more so, aporias for which no solutions – neither optimal nor unambiguous nor definitive – ever come. The responses are multiple, the indications different. There is nothing to prevent the problem presenting itself anew as soon as some expedient is found. In Greek, *aporía* designates scarcity, uncertainty, penury, lack of means. It is the condition of the traveller who, walking through some impervious terrain, finds the path blocked and does not know how to proceed. Aporia is the puzzlement that assails this traveller; but it is also the difficulty of whoever has pushed themselves to the limit. The same goes for those who philosophise and radically interrogate time, the beginning, the end, but also themselves. The philosophical question begins the opening of possibility, the aporia of 'perhaps like that' or 'maybe otherwise' which the responsibility of the decision requires.

The aporia is, therefore, destined to remain both the cue to philosophy and the wound it leaves. The question rests in the core of the response, thus preventing any conclusion. For instance, the closure that would be provided by an extorted confession or some forced statement. But to ask questions is not to mount an inquisition, and it is the question, not the answer, that imposes itself. She who philosophises abandons herself to the passion of the question, without any pretence of showing her hand. In the conclusion of his famous essay *The Question Concerning Technology*, Heidegger writes 'das Fragen ist die Frömmigkeit des Denkens', usually translated 'questioning is the piety of thought'.[2] Still, these words end up assuming a religious connotation, rendering their meaning incomprehensible. But Heidegger himself suggests the semantic proximity of *fromm* to *fügsam*, which means 'docile'. The docility of those who cede and acquiesce to the question: here lies the secret of thought.

In turn, the question is itself put into question. Nor does this doubling, this splitting, spare the questioner. In its radicality, the philosophical question interrogates also the questioner, removing her from her position, dethroning her from that post, deposing her from the pulpit from which she was interrogating and making her one of the interrogated. Philosophy, the philosopher, cannot escape this continual questioning, which is also, in a certain sense, a deposition and a splitting.

It can thus be said that this doubling, this splitting of philosophy – which always takes the form of a question to the question – is the abyssal place where, rejecting any sovereignty, philosophy accepts its own unfolding in order not to fall into the abyss.

13

The out-of-place of metaphysics

Every discipline has some dominion where it reigns sovereign, whose borders it jealously defends. This goes also for the humanistic disciplines, even if they are ever more debased and displaced by the neurobiological sciences, manipulated by cognitive simulation, reduced to calculation. So, what of philosophy?

Philosophy's atopia, the out-of-place which inhabits it, from the outset consigns it to a paradoxical territory where every vain hope of sovereignty must be overthrown. Philosophy cannot be situated or institutionalised. The atopic condition is an oxymoron which reveals the unconditional of philosophy.

This paradoxical territory, out-of-place and impossible to assign, is given a corresponding name: metaphysics. This is, in the last analysis, a non-name for a science which cannot be localised, circumscribed, identified, one which evades any classification, perhaps even a non-science more than a science without a name.

The history is well known. When, in the first century so preoccupied with salvaging and promoting what remained of the Greek tradition, Andronicus of Rhodes sought to use his philological know-how to put Aristotle's body of work in order, he found himself in great difficulty when it came to the fourteen books which constituted his main *oeuvre*, coming after the ones on physics. He thus called them *tà metàà tàà phusiká*, literally, 'that which [neuter plural] comes after physics'. But the Greek preposition *metá* has a double meaning: both 'after' and 'beyond'. This fortuitous editorial label, perhaps intended to be temporary, ended up designating philosophy, precisely in its atopic character. Thus, according to Kant, even if this choice of label was accidental, it cannot be considered entirely a matter of chance – which is as if to say that there was some motivation for it. Heidegger detected a fundamental embarrassment within the origin of this term: the puzzlement felt by Andronicus who, in the Hellenistic tripartition of philosophy into logic, physics and ethics, could not find the right place for the study of beings, which is to say, the first philosophy.[1]

This title thus harboured a fundamental question, destined to drive discussion for centuries. It asked whether beyond the physical world there is concealed a world truer than the real one limited to appearances. This question does not so much concern the 'after' as the 'beyond'. Indeed, one need only glance at those books to understand that what the *Metaphysics* discusses, even if it comes after physics or other disciplines in the itinerary of human understanding, nonetheless comes before law, for it regards being itself. Such disputes as do take place revolve rather more around the 'beyond'. What on earth would it mean to speak of a world beyond the world? A back-world? A hidden world? Would this not be a no-man's-land, a land of dreams, a kingdom amidst the clouds, frequented by adventurers and inhabited by visionaries?

Diffidence is ancient; it emerged together with philosophy itself. For the attitude of those who do not settle for what exists – who think that the physical world is not everything, and are thus driven to go beyond it – has from the outset been metaphysical. Philosophy springs from dissatisfaction at that which immediately offers itself up to the senses, at the simply given. From the outset, therefore, philosophy is metaphysical. The movement which seeks to go beyond also marks out the tendency to unify and order that which is dispersed and multiple. The philosopher's gaze scrutinises beings in order to seek out their genesis, to recognise their *phúsis*, at first identified with some natural element. For Thales, it was water; for others, air, fire, earth. The part stands in for the whole, and one of the natural elements emerges as the principle for explaining the world. And thus, it is an aporia which remains overly linked to the apparent world. The gaze thus grows sharper, pushing further beyond: for Empedocles the explanatory principle is mixture, for Anaximander the *ápeiron* – the unlimited – for Democritus the atom, while for his part Pythagoras had already indicated it in numbers. Thus, there is a movement toward the ever-less tangible.

Even Socrates, who stepped away from investigations of nature, is suspected of pushing beyond. Rather, in his case, the condemnation was even graver. The famous comedian Aristophanes accused him of wallowing among the clouds. And precisely because Socrates himself issued the invitation not to trust appearances, to look beyond immediacy, the accusation was not without justification. It would hang over philosophy like a sword of Damocles.

But who isn't tempted by the adventure into the unknown? Who isn't attracted by what is lying in wait beyond the barrier of the senses and of the present? Metaphysics would, then, be the abandonment of the solid, fruitful, easily cultivated fields of experience; it would be an irresponsible escape, a desertion of judgement and reason. And all that just for the sake of chasing the temptations of mystery, the seductions of the unknowable. Metaphysicians have no territory if not the rocky, unreachable summits, with their rarefied abstractions, and the boundless oceans of unverifiable theories, where the only certain thing is shipwreck.

The discredit that strikes at metaphysics impacts philosophy, too. It is impossible to spell out all the multiple shifts of meaning the term 'metaphysics' has undergone over more than two millennia. But it all revolves around the preposition *metá*, whose fertile ambivalence harbours the out-of-place of philosophy. This is not only a matter of hermeneutical attempts, but also of true and proper efforts to frustrate that dangerous atopia, that troubling exception. That means efforts to territorialise metaphysics, driving the *metá* either toward an empirical 'after' or a mystical 'nether-world'. In the first case, metaphysics is made to bend to ontology, the logic of beings, one science among others, whose content may be observed from different perspectives and further specified, circumscribed, hollowed out. In the second case, the realm of that which lies beyond the senses is walled off, hidden behind that which is tangible and real. With a drastic semantic narrowing, 'metaphysical' becomes synonymous with all that which exceeds the phenomenal world 'on this side', thus indicating the doctrine of the otherworldly, theology. Here, too, it is delimited and defined starting out from the earth and the need to situate that which appears without-a-place. The whole philosophical tradition could be reinterpreted through the prism of these two opposed tendencies, which end up erasing the value of the 'beyond' conserved within the Greek preposition.

The offensive arrives from the territories of 'physics', which seeks to impose itself as the only positive terrain of the knowable. And the attack becomes all the harsher the more the barriers are strengthened by the progress of the individual disciplines and the success of the experimental method. The truth that lies out of reach is substituted by the truth over on this side. Preoccupied by philosophy's rearguard position, Kant shows reason its own limits: better not to venture beyond experience, better not to chase the dream of metaphysics, which would risk fooling oneself and taking for reality one's own chimeras, empty visions and castles in the sky. The situation is even more tragic than one would think, for Kant manages to breathe new life into philosophy only at the cost of an ascesis of the limit. There would long be speculation on this limit. But the true enemy of metaphysics is positivism, that limited and obtuse way of reasoning which peddles the present as the only possible world, the firm ground of the *res bene finita*, the realm of the intact and inalterable.

Philosophy's flight from the 'metaphysical dream', which has been almost unstoppable since the death of Hegel, is explained by this discredit, this systematic delegitimisation which, reaching its peak in the last century, turns metaphysics into a useless and obscure abstraction. Not by accident, the bitterest hostility appeared among the logical neopositivists. Rudolf Carnap's polemical 1931 text *The Elimination of Metaphysics through Logical Analysis of Language* is still famous today. As legend has it, in the Vienna Circle whenever someone wanted to demolish some argument they would exclaim 'metaphysics!', by this meaning that it was so abstruse as to become absurd, departing from the realm of the knowable. The more philosophy became a handmaiden of science, the more metaphysics was destined to disappearance. 'Postmetaphysical thought' like Habermas's is nothing but a Kant-style renunciation of the beyond, a steadfast assertion of a low-key rationality that unfolds at the level of immanence.

Different is the attitude adopted by Heidegger. While in his critique of metaphysics he, too, heralds its end, he also raises the question in the most radical of ways. Conceived as a science of beings (*Seiendes*), metaphysics has lost its reference to Being (*Sein*), the source, the wellspring from which every being comes. Being has been reduced to *a* being, even if the most important of beings. This oblivion of Being is inscribed within metaphysics, and the existential and political effects are devastating. For each risks living dispersed among beings, prey to an ontic sleep. This is all the more true in modernity, where metaphysics has assumed the dark and metallic face of technology, the gyration of the cogs which promises no escape. On closer inspection, Heidegger is sounding an alarm. And he does this not only by attributing enormous importance to metaphysics, but also by indicating the decisive point in the reference to the beyond. The erosion of the beyond is, at root, the cause which has determined the oblivion of Being.

But even if the beyond has been interminably put on hold, this does not mean that it has disappeared. And unless it wants to self-destruct, philosophy is a thinking of the beyond. The point is how to interpret it. In a few pages at the end of his 'Tübinger Einleitung in die Philosophie', Ernst Bloch proposes a rereading of the name 'metaphysics', which is, at the same time, also its redemption. Metaphysics would, for Bloch, indicate *das Offene*, 'the open' – there where there is the secret, that immanent enigma, which has not yet been unravelled.[2] Bloch recognises that the beyond has to do not with the intangible, but with the out-of-place, with that elsewhere which is not yet there, with utopia. An ontology of not-yet-being takes form. The passage from metaphysics to utopian ontology is achieved thanks to a transcending without transcendence.

14

Dissent and critique

Besides its own limits, the question 'what is philosophy?' also gives rise to a great variety of responses. This would hardly happen in the case of physics, chemistry, medicine, or even of history. In the kingdom of knowledge, there is a determinate place for each of these subject-matters – even admitting the possibility that they may shift around somewhat.

But if one asked a philosopher to clarify and explain what philosophy is, the result would be uncertain. Each would provide their own version. To appeal to recognised authorities, from Plato to Husserl, would not diminish this uncertainty; rather, it would only add to the confusion. Is it a science? Some say it is one – and would even add that it is an exact science, while others consider it rather more a synthesis of the sciences, or perhaps, better, an auxiliary discipline. On the opposite side, voices would be raised sharply denying this: far from being a science, philosophy is akin to art and contiguous with literature. For the diehards – and there are no few of them – it is intimately connected to poetry.

A quarrel would also break out over method. The partisans of experience would be challenged by the friends of intuition, the logicians by the hermeneuticians. And then one gets to the raw nerve of personal style: does the philosopher have a neutral tone, because she is speaking of 'objective facts', or does she have an individual stamp, given that her thought cannot be separated from life itself? The discussion would then end with the substance of philosophy. There is no agreement here, either. Does philosophy concern itself with internal and universal laws, or with formal propositions? Is it a 'creation of concepts', as Deleuze and Guattari maintain, or does it instead unmask them, reducing them to a 'mobile army of metaphors', as Nietzsche so acutely suggested?[1]

Precisely because there is no consensus even on the principles of the discipline – which are not truly 'principles', much as, upon closer inspection, philosophy is not a 'discipline' – the contest among philosophers, which is not held in check by the delimitation of any terrain of dispute, is tough and implacable. The exponents of different schools and approaches do not recognise one another. One can arrive even at complete rejection. This does not mean accusing others' theses of being false, but rather of expelling them beyond the confines of philosophy entirely. For an American analytic philosopher, it is beyond doubt that a European deconstructionist can do nothing more than teach comparative literature. While there are some driven by peaceful intentions who seek to reconcile distant theories and dialectically transcend opposites – perhaps even with the none-too-well-hidden aim of integrating them into their own theory – especially in recent decades there have also been many more rigid attitudes. The exclusion takes place even before there is any engagement. That is why, now more than ever, one ought not take for granted the meaning of 'philosophy'.

Philosophers' internal quarrels also present themselves to the outside world, except that now they are exponentially harshened and amplified. It should be admitted: philosophers do not have good relations with the community in which they live. Ever since the times of the trial against Socrates, the tension has never dissipated. How could it be otherwise? It is hard to understand what philosophers' usefulness is meant to be, what contribution they offer to the common good. Ultimately, one would gladly do without such airy chatter, where philosophers claim everything and its opposite, and do without such tiresome, maddening drivel which, even in the best of cases, leaves one empty-handed and with a big headache. It would be better to read a good novel. The alternative is an intervention by a scientist, who – even apart from the prestige and authority they enjoy – has the irrefutable merit of resolving, or helping to resolve, some concrete, specific problem that springs from some need of humanity. Even in the case that the scientist dedicates herself to apparently useless investigation or probes some obscure theme, her life devoted to science nonetheless makes her a hero of progress, garlanding her in an aura of venerability.

Matters are very different when it comes to philosophy, which can boast no success and claim no discoveries. And besides, there's no Nobel Prize for philosophy. Henri Bergson, Bertrand Russell and Jean-Paul Sartre did each receive one, in 1927, 1950 and 1964 respectively, but they were awarded the prize for literature; more recently, in 1998 Amartya Sen got the Nobel Prize for economics. The results for which Descartes or Leibniz might be acknowledged belong to the realm of mathematics; those achieved by Hume to psychology, and Ernst Mach's to physics. It was not their philosophical ideas that secured them prizes and recognition.

The point is that philosophers are not called on in the community to resolve problems – if not out of a misunderstanding. Indeed, they are not able to indicate any solution; rather, it is they who raise questions, one after another, who pose problems even where, in others' eyes, there would not appear to be any. Can any more thankless, unrewarding role be imagined? Those who philosophise do perhaps tend to show a certain indifference toward the community's judgement. But it should be granted that, as they are struck from multiple fronts, both internally and externally, they may well end up becoming exasperated. Their estrangement from the world becomes more acute: already marginal, they marginalise themselves. And they thus live in concealment, to preserve not so much their freedom as the radicality of their thought. From the village of Voorburg where Spinoza managed to concentrate his efforts on his *Ethics*, to the smoky London rooms where Marx wrote his *Capital*, from the refuge of Todtnauberg where Heidegger finished *Being and Time* to the chalet on the Norwegian fjord where Wittgenstein found a little calm, the great masterpieces of philosophy have seen the light of day in solitude, distant from the *agorá*, but in latent, strenuous tension.

On many past occasions, this hidden tension ultimately concluded in overt persecution. How could one forget the flames in which Giordano Bruno was burned alive on Rome's Campo de' Fiori on 17 February 1600 – another dramatic, mournful scene? Bringing to mind the death of Socrates, it provided a modern, even crueller and more ruthless version of the insuperable tension between the philosopher and the community. It's true: no few scientists entered into conflict with their own world because of their theories, too advanced for the times, and ended up as victims of abuse and oppression. Emblematic is the case of Galileo, who is always cited alongside Bruno. But as Jaspers has observed, the different outcomes – in one case abjuration, in the other burning at the stake – attest to two different types of truth. Galileo did not have to jeopardise his life just for the sake of a scientific truth which, being universally valid and made of rigour and precision, would have affirmed itself even without any personal involvement on his part. On the contrary, Bruno had to accept death for philosophical truth, absolute in its uniqueness.[2] If, moreover, one considers the Galileo affair more closely, it becomes clear that the cornerstone of the scandal was not his heliocentric theory itself. Indeed, he was free to publicly uphold such a theory, so long as he inserted it, as the Jesuits demanded, within the traditional theological-philosophical framing. It is no accident that heliocentrism had found adepts already centuries earlier, even within ecclesiastical ranks.[3] What drew the persecutors' wrath onto Galileo's head was not his scientific theories but rather the philosophical conceptions within which they were framed. All this is even more obvious today. Scientific theories impose themselves autonomously. Even if they did run into the censorship of some intolerant regime, they would be admitted elsewhere, recognised and acclaimed. The scientist may be a dissident – but for political, religious or philosophical reasons, not for scientific ones. The tension between the scientist and the community is occasional and, in the last analysis, only apparent.

On the contrary, the tension between the philosopher and the community is radical and irrevocable. Despite everything, philosophy has never lost its original disruptive charge, its critical potential. The resistance it puts up to reality springs from its own atopia, which renders every *arché*, every principle, fundamentally an-archic. From the form of life to scientific concepts, from modes of action to widespread habits, nothing escapes its vigilant gaze, which sifts through not only traditions but also that which has become so obvious as to seem natural, immutable, eternal. In the sphere of existence as in the sphere of politics, philosophy points an accusing figure against the self-evident.

Of course, with its inventions and its technological repercussions, science, too, has shaken up what was once customary, drastically and perhaps irreversibly transforming human life. Yet, scientific rationalisation has helped to consolidate old illusions or even to forge new ones, while technology, in introducing simplifying processes, has ended up condemning the capacities of the intellect to regression if not outright disappearance. This paradoxical reversal forbids any rash move to chalk up for progress all that science has to offer. The inherent limitedness of its horizon – that rationalism of the particular that can give rise to the most senseless destructiveness – shows, more than ever, the need for a thought like philosophy's, that does not subject itself to criteria of usefulness, does not subordinate itself to some purpose, but always looks beyond. To critique does not mean – as some would have it – to cavil or condemn.[4] Rather, critique is that theoretical and practical commitment which never accepts anything without reflection. Uncomfortable, controversial, devoid of any unambiguous criteria and without stringent proofs, philosophy has never abandoned its aspiration to grasp the connections, make out the links between all that appears single and separate. Fundamentally, this is the demand advanced by Plato when he maintains that it should be philosophers who govern the *pólis* – that is, those who are capable of combining different capacities, of uniting otherwise disparate understandings, in each case grasping knowledge in the widest of perspectives.

15

The twentieth century: breaks and traumas

The twentieth century represents one of philosophy's high points across its over 2,500-year history. It was characterised by an unprecedented radicality. This was expressed in the acute, sometimes inflamed critique of reason and in the attempt to deconstruct the Western tradition.

The break from the past – so keenly felt at the dawn of the century – marks a watershed in the stream of thought. Yet, nor could one deny the continuity with today, which no recent event – the Chernobyl disaster, the fall of the Berlin Wall, September 11, or the global pandemic – seems to have scratched. It is as if the last century had continued even beyond the start of the new millennium, which has not been marked either by a change of course or by the irruption of new contents. It can thus be said that the twentieth century, understood as an epoch, has not yet reached its conclusion.

Over the centuries, the individual disciplines have separated out from the Queen of the Sciences. Yet, even in the eighteenth century, physics and cosmology remained within its orbit. What happened subsequently, by means of growing specialisation, was its definitive abandonment

by the sciences, culminating in the twentieth century with
the breaking-off of psychology and sociology. The Queen
is thus left all by herself. Ever more nomadic and stateless,
she is called on to intervene in distant fields and on disparate questions. Her inventory widens, encompassing the
concepts which have remained unthought.[1]

The extreme radicality of twentieth-century thought
is also to be explained in light of the catastrophic events
that pockmarked the century: the two world wars, the
Holocaust and Hiroshima. Reflection on modernity took its
cue not only from the unprecedented innovation, from the
extraordinary scientific progress, from the explosive results
achieved by technology, but also from incomparable processes of destruction and self-destruction. Philosophy was
profoundly shaken, lacerated, afflicted by all this. All the
more so given that it had already detected some of these outcomes. It became a critical voice – but no longer in the name
of Reason. Its target, rather, was the technological rationality of the Western world. It was necessary to re-question
old concepts which had ossified over time and to demolish
old idols that had passed with impunity into the repertoire
of the sciences, producing crimes and misadventures.

Philosophy felt the weight of this responsibility. 'The
innocence of a neutral self-understanding was all over after
1945 anyway.'[2] Whereas soldiers, politicians and scientists
tried to exonerate themselves or escape scrutiny, most philosophers declared their own guilt. Not without tensions,
conflicts and paradoxes. But to admit the crime of thought,
a heavy charge ever since the times of Plato, did not mean
succeeding in thinking crime itself, which ended up long
being relegated into the sacral and intangible sphere of
Evil. The shadows built up troublingly and the already
problematic relationship with power became yet more
tense and conflicted. The voice of women, who finally
came out onto the front of the philosophical stage, helped
to articulate political reflection with a new stamp.

But the question that remains open is how one should
interpret a century which, precisely because of its con-

tinuity, still arouses passions today and does not allow
the due distance, the 'cold-bloodedness' with which, as
Hegel suggests, one ought to consider history. Thus,
in this inextricable tangle it seems difficult to identify
the image of the time in any single event, theme or
character. There is no lack of candidates: the Russian
Revolution, the atom bomb, the theory of relativity, the
moon landing, the sexual revolution. Not even the dark
hyperbole of the Holocaust, the extermination of the
Jews of Europe – still not investigated in all its conceptual depth – could fully shed light on the global drama
of the twentieth century.

This is why in his recent book *What Happened in the
Twentieth Century?*, Sloterdijk rejects all those labels
which have made some headway thus far: from the 'age
of totalitarianisms' – which would offer only a partial and
exemplifying picture – to the 'short century' – a formula
which attempts to make the whole twentieth century coin-
cide with the history of the Soviet experiment, running from
1917 to 1990.[3] It is as if the 'great global civil war' between
communism and fascism could exhaust the meaning of
such a complex century. Sloterdijk suggests throwing off
the old schemas and finding a point of entry into this
self-destruction. The risk, above all for Europeans, would
be that they put behind them a 'lost century' which, with
its conflicts and atrocities, appears as a desolate scrapyard
of violence and an arsenal of myths which some would still
be inclined to draw from.

To Sloterdijk's eyes, the twentieth century appears not
only as the outcome of modernity, but also as the advance of
'big politics', characterised by extremism. Eric Hobsbawm
would then be right to speak of an 'Age of Extremes'.[4]
But for Sloterdijk, it is something more than this. Thus,
he attaches the twentieth century to an 'apocalypse of the
real'. This – only apparently enigmatic – formula alludes to
the 'passion of the real' with which Alain Badiou defined
the tension of this epoch in his essay *The Century*. The two
interpretations are opposed, specular.[5]

The here and the now: the will to realise one's own projects immediately. A century of resistances and great epics, a remorseless destroyer, the twentieth century sought, through its works, to match the real for which it had such passion. But if for Badiou this passion still has some value, for Sloterdijk it is time to ruthlessly examine and unmask it. The passion for the real was the way of reacting to an unbearable complexity. The twentieth century ought to be seen as a furious battle 'in the name of the real', fought with an attitude both proud and severe, out of the aspiration for a radical rupture with the world that went before.

But perhaps it was precisely the opposite. If the twentieth century left so many spectres in circulation, that is because it put on the agenda so many dreams that were not realised. That is why it cannot be forgotten or overlooked. The task for the new century, which does not want to live in a torpor troubled by spectres, must, then, be a new interpretation of dreams.

16

After Heidegger

Can one speak of a politics in Heidegger? There are two risks in answering such a question: either denying point-blank, or else making only cursory reference to the fatal embrace he made in 1933. The need to break out of this alternative, which was posed already before the *Black Notebooks*, has now become impossible to put off any longer.[1]

Philosophy can end up in a vicious circle here – or more precisely, philosophy is already in part finished, considering some of the effects it had. The greater the distance one gains from it, the clearer the symbolic character of the 'Heidegger case', which goes beyond his figure and even his thought. For this twentieth-century drama brings to mind the ancient one; and in the background, there stands out a double image which sometimes assumes the traits of Socrates, at other times the traits of Plato. Is this the repeat of an unfair trial against the philosopher, this time not in a courthouse but rather – as a sign of the times – a trial by media? Or was it the philosopher who ventured into a stormy sea?

In either case, after centuries of absence philosophy was so brazen as to enter back into the city. And once again it lost its challenge for power, becoming subaltern by way of an incautious and rash alliance. But on closer inspection, philosophy did not make its entrance into the city; rather, it allowed politics to burst into the university classrooms, and not without violence. One cannot, however, limit the problem to the dangers of political activism, which, after all, seduced more than one philosopher over the course of the last century (one need only think of Sartre). In the 'Heidegger case' the tension between philosophy and politics re-emerges in the most exasperated terms. And it would be short-sighted not to perceive its effects on current affairs. A lesson for the present and the future was, more or less tacitly, drawn from what had happened in the past. For after that humiliation, after that ignominious defeat – perhaps the most burning and dispiriting of setbacks – philosophy seemed destined to bear the weight of its unhappy consciousness, shrewdly limiting itself within academic confines, outside of politics. Even insofar as it did intervene in politics, it adapted itself to a role as the functionary or, better, the press officer for democracy. Hence why one cannot understand the contemporary panorama without casting some light on the 'Heidegger case'.

It is no surprise that within the bequest left by such an acute and alert philosopher as Hans Blumenberg, a file was found containing various manuscripts dedicated to the role of philosophy in the contemporary world. The protagonist is Heidegger, the title *Die Verführbarkeit des Philosophen*.[2] In its complex ambivalence, this expression indicates both the appeal of the seductive philosopher, and the possibility that, thanks to his availability, the seducer was himself seduced, fascinated, pushed to drive or perversely imagine that he was 'driving the driver' – and the expression *den Führer führen* also recurs in this work. Philosophy's relationship with power is intricate, counterproductive, harmful, perhaps lethal. Heidegger *docet*. For the twentieth century and beyond, he became the hyperbolic symbol of a historic defeat, all the more deplorable because already heralded in the past, a sort of Stalingrad for philosophy, impossible to forget. One can thus grasp why the undeclared trial, especially in German universities, extends also to Nietzsche, Hegel, Fichte, Rousseau – and even drags in Plato, again hauled into the dock. And lastly even Socrates, accused of not having been 'democratic' and thus having deserved condemnation.

Heidegger, like Plato. This short-circuit was established already by Heidegger's direct pupils, who introduced this comparison as an apology – one of doubtful success. The first was Arendt who, in her controversial 1969 essay 'Martin Heidegger at Eighty', spoke of a 'false step', a 'temptation to get involved in the world of human affairs'. She further adds, as an excuse, that 'the attraction to the tyrannical can be demonstrated theoretically in many of the great thinkers'.[3] Gadamer followed her years later in an article with the eloquent title 'Back from Syracuse?'[4] Beyond suggesting a rather questionable comparison – and passing off adherence to Nazism as an accidental error – this image reasserts the cliché of the philosopher who, giving in to the temptation to realise his ideas, both causes damage and himself ends up the victim. Better, then, not to venture outside of thought's own proper abode.

The popular-liberal stereotype of the philosopher incompetent in matters of politics was destined for great success.[5] Arendt and Gadamer were, moreover, the first liberal Heideggerians. Concealed within the foundations of this stereotype was a little-edifying conception not only of philosophy, but also of politics: the former abstract, rigid, characterised by a 'tyrannical' trait; the latter concrete and simple, resistant to ideas and ideals. It would, then, be appropriate, indeed, necessary, to establish a separation between them. It should be added that neither Arendt nor Gadamer themselves complied with this obligation; but both renounced any critique of liberal democracy. In different forms, they were exponents of a new tendency which has taken root since the immediate postwar period: the bid to democratise democracy. It was this that marked their distance from Heidegger, whose reflection concentrated on the critique of liberal democracy.

That is why, even when retrospectively evaluating the events of recent decades, the image of Syracuse ought to be rebuffed. Not only does it banalise the 'Heidegger case' but it suggests that philosophy – having openly declared its own incompetence – should stay out of politics or, at most, run along behind in an ancillary role, providing backup and support for liberal democracy. If the philosopher may make mistakes in individual choices of active politics, the question here is not limited to his supposed amateurish incapacity.

To provide a synthesis of Heidegger's error, one can speak of a political territorialisation of atopia. This is especially contradictory considering that Heidegger is the philosopher of statelessness. His refuge in the Black Forest was profoundly deterritorialised. Yet, such a location was no longer a matter of indifference. In denouncing the double risk of the planetary age – that is, naive autochthony and technological mobility – Heidegger delineated a phenomenology of habitation, understood as migration; atopia is not the world's outside, but rather a well-thought being-in-the-world. And there's more: Heidegger chose philosophy as a reflexive practice of atopia, and with his anarchitectures shook the very foundations of tradition.

A messenger from a cityless clime, Heidegger set off down a little-beaten track to lead politics back to the place to which its etymology calls it – to the *pólis*. He interprets it, outside of the old state schemas, as the pole around which existence revolves: the 'seat' of the human sojourn and of a cohabitation which is yet to come. Far from the instrumental conception of politics for which he reproached Schmitt, he did not look to *arché*, to the principle in the most imperial sense – for *imperium* means command – that would order the community. *Pólis* is rather more the place of the *Ereignis*, of the event which discloses history and thus escapes any metaphysics. Heidegger rethinks the *pólis* not from an impolitical stance, but rather by refusing the urban vision of politics, the exchange of opinions at the marketplace, the debate in the parliamentary assembly. The site from which he speaks is extra-parliamentary and ultra-parliamentary. His access to the political space can take place only by way of the state of exception promised to an unredeemed world. In this sense, his politics is a poetry of emergency.[6]

After the *Black Notebooks*, anyone would be hard-pressed to maintain that Heidegger was inattentive to the events of his era. The image of the philosopher at ease in an apolitical conformism is bound to fall apart. On the contrary, Heidegger was a radical philosopher, an acute clinician, a far-sighted diagnostic who hit the mark when he recognised that the planet was the new landscape for politics. The planetarised *pólis* is the enigma that must in future be unravelled. Can one still use the term 'politics' for this spatiality? Heidegger prefers to speak of 'planetarism'. In such a context, rather than limit himself to a meagre critique, he indicated the advance of capital in *Gestell*, in the *dispositif* of technology. He bequeathed the task of deconstructing this engine of the archi-economy.

In a strongly apocalyptic vision, Heidegger not only pushes forth along the abyssal confines of the Occident – that 'Land of Sunset' which has now entered into the nocturnal age of destitution – but also looks to the time in which the end of history obsessively repeats itself and allows no other beginning. It could then be said that 'the explorer is the author of the theorem of post-history'.[7] But what of those whose existence already falls outside of any history that makes sense, consumed as it is in the blinding life-forms of the technological world, in the dark post-historical smoke of advanced capitalism? Heidegger's philosophy of history is, therefore, an eschatology, a reflection on the *éschaton*, on the extreme limit, a thought which is in turn extreme, which seeks a crossing-point, a passageway. Passing beyond, turning point, revolution: Heidegger redesigns a kinetics of philosophy and politics. He critiques revolution – holding it to be still too metaphysical – to which he opposes the event. But this master of the vertical fall, of thrownness and of fallenness, did not find the path of exodus. Obstinately remaining within the intimate and the private, he chose the wrong revolution – the 'brown' one. When this became the knowledge of catastrophe, he entrusted it both to Hölderlin – who nurtured the dreamt-of and never-fulfilled revolution in the ontological depth of poetry – and on the other hand to his disciples, the 'strangers of the same heart', few, rare and troubled, the next to come after.

The fact that Heidegger territorialised atopia does not mean that the anarchitectures of his thought were thereby cancelled out, or that his deterritorialised legacy was erased. Still less does it mean that atopia is a danger, a hazard that philosophers ought to void.

17

Against negotiators and normative philosophers

In recent times, a philosophy of normative stamp has been doing the rounds. Emboldened by a compliant academic capitalism, it has transcended old confines, even though it was born under the skies of analytical inertia. Far from the radicality of twentieth-century thought, this philosophy openly declares itself a *handmaiden* not only of science, but also of politics – or better, of economics.

Thus, the philosopher who recognises herself in this tendency admits that she is a 'negotiator'. The term, drawn from the commercial verbiage of dealing, of trafficking, of trading, here comes to indicate – in a wider juridical context – the negotiations that precede a diplomatic accord or an economic contract. This itself clearly indicates the role that is claimed for it. The philosopher, who has no articles to peddle that are in demand on today's market, can at least offer herself as a 'conceptual negotiator'. What does this mean? Well, if a society's political order changes, and it turns from a monarchy into a republic, the negotiator-philosopher can help to define the concept of citizen. If some new scientific discovery is being celebrated, for instance if water has been found on Mars, in this case, too, it will be perhaps be of service to pose the question of what a planet is, and 'conceptual talks' will be of use. Conceptual negotiations can help along 'business mergers', set 'diverse company cultures' in dialogue, or indeed evaluate the 'relevance of statistics', and so on. The examples could go on. In short, philosophy has 'good days ahead of it'. Having thrown off its old clothes, it has found these new spaces in which to intervene.[1]

Here, it is supposed that the philosopher does not pose questions, but rather seeks to respond to the questions posed by others. Which means, to resolve the problems that the other disciplines have the merit of posing. So, this is something quite different than Being, History, Life, and all that kind of chit-chat! Here, one gets down to concrete matters, negotiating the boundaries of concepts, delimiting and circumscribing. This is the unique capacity of the philosopher who, surveying things a little here and a little there, sets herself the task of 'overcoming the tensions'. After all, the negotiation may fail, and then it will be necessary immediately to start again from scratch. For what counts, here, is to arrive at a solution.

In this commercial vision of philosophy, which is completely subaltern to science, to politics, to economics, everything plays out within the terms of a cost-benefit analysis. The negotiator-philosopher who declares herself 'neutral' – for otherwise she would be unable to mediate – addresses herself to 'possibility consumers', offering potential options. Indeed, philosophy is a 'conditionals factory'.[2] She wants only to help the 'possibility consumer' reconcile himself with his own decisions – another way of describing the 'care of the self'. Sprung from an exogenous conceptual tension, philosophy hastens to heal this rift and, satisfied with a job well done, it retreats in good order, ready for the next negotiation.

Thus, despite its avowed 'handmaiden' function – 'it serves something else, it depends on something else' – philosophy has proven able to find a place for itself, however indecorous, in the age of advanced capitalism. So, there is no lack of work: if it is, indeed, a conceptual negotiation, then this practice is everywhere widespread. The negotiator-philosopher, the latest firefighter with the soul of an artist, puts out every blaze, mitigates every clash, pacifies all tension. Could she be any gentler or kindlier? Her offer, the goods she peddles, are well compensated by the academy. Yet, that is the very place she seeks to leave behind in order to avoid being cut adrift outside of reality, which is where she aspires to intervene through her labour of mediation.

Mental experiments, riddles, fables, quizzes – these are the methods the negotiator devises in order to give form to her intuitions, but above all to seek to be open, attractive, communicative with the general public. This, it is claimed, is the way to make philosophy accessible for everyone. The experiment doubtless boasts a more than respectable history. Yet it was born in a laboratory, and puts its own provenance on show. How could one forget Galileo, with whom it first began? Or the latest big scientific discoveries? The experiment conducted in the laboratory is checked, verified, confirmed – until there is some proof to the contrary. Indeed, one can even repeat the experiment multiple times, until it is finally crowned with success. It aims at understanding, which, moreover, can always be rectified and perfected. But what sense does it make to artificially introduce this method – so optimal for science – into philosophy? Hidden in the foundations of this improper transposition is the confusion between experiment and experience. The subject of the experiment, sat in her aseptic laboratory, is sovereign: she abstracts, isolates, repeats, checks. But the verb proper to philosophy is 'to experience'. There is no dominating subject. On the contrary, they who experience are dominated, proven wrong, disoriented. That is why people say, 'I've also had this experience', which means 'I wasn't expecting it, and I had to learn.' There is an unmistakeable element of negativity. Suddenly, everything changed:

not only the world, now seen in a new light, but also those who underwent this experience. In his *Phenomenology of Spirit*, Hegel describes this transformation as a 'reversal of consciousness'. Nothing could be further from mental experiments, accessible only to willing laboratory staff; whoever desires reflection on their own existence will steer clear of them.

No less abstruse and artificial are the pseudo-fables which – considering their recent uses and abuses – can have devastating effects. The principle here is analogous to the principle of the experiment. These fables are apparently realistic, yet they are entirely fictional and abstract. They would have us believe that existence is a laboratory of experiments where one can test the most absurd hypotheses without any great risk through argumentative games and elucubrations. What does it matter, then, if it is a problem of life and death? Everything is banalised in a ludic version of ethics, which has very little ethical about it.

A famous example is the trolley problem, the fable of the 'fat man' – which is meant to be told with a certain playful tone, and prompt mirth.[3] An out-of-control rail carriage is hurtling at full speed toward five men tied to the tracks. From a railway bridge 'you' are overlooking the imminent tragedy. But standing beside you is a stranger, a fat man. If you push him onto the tracks, his body will stop the carriage. Five lives will be saved, but he will die. So, would you kill the fat man?

In the trolleyology which has built up around this problem, experts have entertained themselves thinking up all the possible solutions. But the question is: why on earth would I find myself on that bridge? Faced with such an improbable scene? How come, just with the word 'you', the person telling the story can sneakily rope in the interlocutor, pushing them not into a choice but into an ethical transgression? Indeed, whatever they choose, they will be a murderer. Another of these dilemmas is the ticking time bomb, the fable of the terrorist caught by police who has set a time bomb somewhere. Here, 'you' are called to decide whether you would prefer to massacre a hundred-odd people or, more likely, grant the police permission to torture the suspect.

These fables set up a cartoonish world where one must inevitably choose between one evil and another, through a utilitarian cost-benefit calculation: less an ethics of capitalism than a capitalism of ethics. Moral dilemmas of this kind can be compared to the logical analysis of propositions. Acceptable as textbook exercises, they are inadmissible wherever they purport to have any influence over reality. What needs to be rejected, here, is not only one solution or another, but the question itself. To luxuriate in debates of this kind, as this neuroeconomics does, is a legitimate pastime, however idle it is – but it is not entirely harmless. Indeed, it imposes an authoritarian ultimatum – kill or allow others to be run over; allow a massacre or else torture – which is not given within the experience of the person called on to make the choice. The torture example itself shows the danger inherent within these pseudo-philosophical fables, which can become a means of ethical and political manipulation.[4]

Whilst more orthodox analytical currents have prevailed within its ranks, normative philosophy has established itself across wide fields, from ethics (in its various branches – bioethics, applied ethics, etc.) to the theory of justice and the debate on rights. Political liberalism, in the paradigmatic version provided by Rawls, which draws deep on mental experiments, has summarised its modalities, contents and intentions.[5] Every question is depoliticised; what instead prevails is a wholly internal moral or moralistic approach. Here, the very things that ought to be an object of critical reflection are instead presupposed. Rather than interrogate asymmetry, it takes its cue from an ideal symmetry between free and equal individuals. It is as if every economic, political or social problem, from exploitation to violence, from corruption to poverty, were always and only due to a lack of freedom. This 'egalitarianism' comes across as all the more strident in a world which continually belies the ideals of independence, distributive justice and individual freedom.

Various elements contributed to the origins of normative philosophy, but two are the most decisive: on the one hand, the impasse of analytic philosophy which, notwithstanding its dominant position in academia, has not succeeded in communicating with the general public, which remains resistant to its abstruse formulations; on the other, the memory of the traumas of the twentieth century, which has marked recent thought. So never again radicalism, and more negotiation, mediation, democratisation, please. The paradox of this philosophy is that, while it presents itself with a benevolent familiar, accessible aspect, its real echo is limited. It can achieve a certain success only if it is backed up by power.

Why should this be? It is not difficult to find the answer. This philosophy, which aspires to be post-twentieth-century, would like to be normal, even more than normative; a discipline among others, or rather, a *handmaiden* to others. It purports to erase its own atopia, almost as if to make up for the past, and no longer to be troubling or estranging. Žižek has rightly spoken of a 'state neo-Kantianism',[6] which gives a good sense of the idea. Especially in the German context, normative philosophy presents itself as a resumption, if not a re-edition, of neo-Kantianism, the academic philosophy which reigned in Marburg before Heidegger swept it away. For their part, the neo-Kantians, from Cohen to Hartmann, passing via Natorp and Cassirer, re-read Kant with the honest – but decidedly well-worn and in some regards myopic – proposal of delineating an ethics, a theory of understanding, an ontology. To re-propose a 'neo-Kantianism' as a style and modality of philosophy today means to present oneself as a bold liberal, able to democratise democracy, overcome the obstacles to communication, mitigate human suffering, provide something that will serve the cause of being a little less unhappy. But these state philosophers have assumed the none-too-well-hidden function of neutralising the effects of science and warding off the disruptive repercussions of technology within the inalienable development of the capitalist economy.

18

Ancilla democratiae: a dejected return

If one had to summarise what has happened over the turn of the millennium, in a transition where continuity has prevailed, one could say that philosophy has entered the city again dejected, wearing sackcloth and ashes. Above all, after the fall of the Berlin Wall and the end of totalitarianism, it is prepared to collaborate with politics, to support democracy and encourage pluralism. Born to Arendt in the era of McCarthyism, the dubious 'two totalitarianisms' thesis has rapidly become a conceptual blockage. As well as forbidding any in-depth reflection either on the peculiarities of Stalinism or on Nazism's political project, it has also offered an alibi for not thinking.[1] The label 'totalitarianism' marks the limit beyond which one may not legitimately venture; it holds up the sign of prohibition which discredits any alternative in advance and represents a perennial admonition.

Mindful of its recent past, philosophy can move, and does move, only on this side of that line, in the domain of democracy. Here, it has a cautiously negative mandate, that of exercising some critique and nurturing a few doubts, denouncing small abuses and irreparable suffering.

But as well as that, it also has an outwardly positive role, namely its commitment in defence of democracy, which is fragile, corrupt, difficult to conquer and impossible to achieve once and for all time. This new condition for philosophy, promoted to an *ancilla democratiae*, is explicated in extreme fashion in Richard Rorty's essay 'The Priority of Democracy over Philosophy'.[2]

Multiple questions could be raised here. But the most important is this one: can a philosopher accord any political form primacy over thought itself? On close inspection, this is what has happened in recent years. Even if he employs an especially hyperbolic formulation, Rorty is hardly alone in this vein. On the one hand, philosophy takes a backward step; seeking to absolve itself, it almost dissolves itself, condemning itself to irrelevance. On the other hand, democracy comes to assume a supremacy which is not so much political as philosophical. It becomes the only possible political form, the only one which is desirable or even thinkable. Philosophy identifies with democracy. All the more so given that – as Derrida repeatedly emphasised – this political form is never realised, but always 'a democracy to come'. The suspicion is that democracy is, in the last analysis, a synonym for public discussion, or even for dialogue itself. This is patently the case in Habermas's theory, where democracy derives from a more foundational principle of discourse, able to encourage participation, safeguard plurality and promote consensus. Political action is channelled, directed toward the communicative terrain, onto which it is called to show its ability to mediate between contrasting ideas, interests and objectives. If politics is not reducible to Schmitt's friend-enemy opposition, nor can one purport to tame all conflict, throwing oneself into a zealous quest for consensus.

At the foundations of this conception it is possible to make out pages from Arendt, interpreted in a tempered key. Doubtless, her reflection on 'judgement' leaves room for more than one critique. Having emphasised the extraneousness of thought, Arendt does not manage to bring

the philosopher back into the city, except on condition
that they are accompanied by the figure of the spectator.
Neither entirely absent – like those who head off elsewhere with their thought – nor entirely present – like
those stuck into the action – the spectator sits in the stalls
(and the scenario is that of the ancient Greek theatre)
as far back as necessary to get an overall view. Between
the thinker – drastically extraneous to common sense –
and the actor – completely immersed in events – there
thus opens up the perspective of the 'spectator' (from the
Greek *theatés*, which links it to 'theory'), whose task lies
in watching the world as if from the outside even while
remaining within it.[3] Her position is shareable: the stalls
are the place where she can compare her own point of
view with others', thus managing to formulate common
judgements. Thought – which would otherwise be vertical
– thus translates into public practice, as it develops in the
shared horizontality.

The spectator would thus open the doors to a new
'political philosophy'.[4] The theatre, as examined from the
spectators' view of things, presents politics as an exchange
of opinions, the encounter among points of view, public
discussion. Hence why this idea cannot be said to be
wholly innocent of ties to the numerous attempts to see
democracy as a practice of consensus. But above all, it
is not innocent when one considers that decisive shift in
philosophy which, in search of toleration in a democratic
regime, has ended up negating itself, condemning itself to a
normative or ameliorative moralism. The project advanced
by Arendt – who, not by accident, always refused to be
called a 'philosopher' – remains at the crossroads between
a nostalgic revisiting of the *pólis* and an effective abandonment of philosophy, a superfluous legitimation of the *après*
which democracy would gladly do without.

The story that comes after is well known: the now-sub-
ordinate philosophy has done nothing but ratify, or every
now and then rectify, an ever-more dilated democracy, on
the one hand imperial in disposition, on the other a formi-

dable *dispositif* for producing consent. Hence the paradox highlighted by Rancière, for whom even as philosophy proclaims its return to the city, it also refutes and belies this very return. This missed rendezvous between philosophy and politics, after the trauma of Socrates' death – which was relived in other forms even in the last century – allows the flourishing of a profound 'disaccord', a genuine incompatibility.[5] The collapse of the totalitarian regimes marked the triumph of democracy. But this success goes hand-in-hand with the hollowing out of democracy, to the point that it becomes ever more formal, ever less political, on the one hand a plaything of the state apparatus, on the other an uninterrupted reporting mechanism directed at sublimating the body of the people in the totality of 'public opinion'. This, moreover, is in line with politics understood as administrative governance or else reduced to police-style management.

And what of philosophy? It would seem to be relegated to scattered night-time thoughts, as it waits for the owl to take flight. Yet the artificially illuminated twilight also looms over politics. Here, everything has become more complicated. For, as if the passage from night to day and day to night no longer took place, democratic consensualism similarly tries to unite the within and the outside, in effect eliding them. This is where philosophy lost any margin of manoeuvre, after anti-utopianism was decreed far and wide. But the so-called 'end of utopias' was merely the unconditional, unlimited, total affirmation of capitalism – an economic order that would not have been able to impose itself without consensual democracy as a political order, entrusted to the sovereign power of the state. Philosophy has accepted that it should no longer set itself too many questions, and still less the most fundamental ones, also because the alternative would be stigmatised as 'totalitarianism' – and the warning has always been explicit. Thus, it has helped to democratise democracy and, within the perspective of a diffuse biopolitical power, it has ended up underestimating the sovereign power of the state. Here, in taking for granted the state dimension of politics, or even just reflecting it, philosophy risks arriving at an impasse. For if thought is always a thought *beyond*, the state does not think.

19

The poetry of clarity

Even philosophy's name is inscribed with the aspiration for clarity. This should not be taken to mean transparency, self-evidence, linearity. A metaphor – no simple one, which opens up a path of profundity in language – can be intensely luminous and suddenly turn on a light.

In the last century, attention to language has become near-obsessive. Philosophy has recognised its own immense debt to words; and recently – with Derrida – also to writing. The search for the right word, the ambition to a peculiar style, has tormented many a philosopher. Others, however, have kept on writing and speaking with utter indifference for language, using it as a simple tool, sometimes even showing disregard toward their interlocutors or addressees. It is not that the fruitful complicity with literature, the mutual penetration with poetry, as promoted by the linguistic turn, have gone away. But it is as if the opaque desire to escape the power of grammar had flourished anew. Thus, it has become something rather rare to read philosophical texts which – without wishing to bypass the 'strenuous effort of the concept' – maintain an evocative and poetic force.

This is, moreover, in harmony with a now-prevalent flight from the word. The specialist codes of science, from biogenetics to molecular chemistry, contribute to this, with their tensor calculus, algebraic conventions, transfinite numbers, calibrations to the nanosecond. But decisive, here, is the newspeak spread by social media, with the homologating jargon, the tribal cryptograms and the hypocritical anti-rhetoric of the blog. New technologies have attacked language at its very heart. Acceleration has dealt a mortal blow, the avalanche of information has debased all semantics. On the one hand, there is a deafening volume of news, on the other an impotent mutism.

Thus it is not difficult to understand that what is also at stake in language is a relationship with power. Indeed, the eclipse of politics is connected to the eclipse of the word. A philosophy which, no longer a handmaiden of science or democracy, prepares itself to speak in the first person about the outside and the beyond, cannot but start again from poetry. The political task is a poetic task.

Plato condemned the poets to expulsion from the *pólis*. He did so not because he judged poetry a vain art, a copy of a world which was, in turn, a copy of ideas (see *Republic* 595a-608c). This was, if anything, an excuse. Rather, he considered Aristophanes, the Attic dramatists, poets in general, responsible for the trial against Socrates, especially because poetry constituted the base of Greek *paideía*, in which Sophistry had taken root. One can understand Plato's disdain. But this philosophical anathema was doubtless an error – and it had deep and lasting repercussions.

A fresh tie between poetry and *pólis* was established thanks to Dante, despite or perhaps thanks to his exile, and it was strengthened in the humanist culture of the Italian city-states.[1] Thus Coluccio Salutati, chancellor of the Florentine Republic, could maintain that the faculty for poetry was the political virtue *par excellence*, because it allowed citizens otherwise immersed in the immediacy of the present to project themselves into the future.[2] The good politician is a poet who marks out new cosmic constellations and unites the community of the *pólis*. The poetic word inaugurates history, and language discloses what a famous expression from Vico, author of a 'poetic politics', called the 'civil world'.[3]

To speak of poetry does not mean to speak of decoration, ornament, verse. If in Italian philosophy the accent falls on the creativity of *poíesis*, in German philosophy, from Hölderlin to Heidegger, the reference is to the German verb *Dichten*, in all its extraordinarily complex meanings. The etymological figure goes back to the Lain *dictare*. More than a gratifying creation produced out of nothingness, poetry is dictated to the poet; accepting this vocation, she exposes herself to the most extreme outside in order to listen to this calling. This alone would be a model for philosophy. But *Dichten* also means to condense. And the most notable convergence perhaps lies here, in the capacity for synthesis. Words do not drop from the clouds, do not descend from the sky. Only with difficulty do they densely gather together: they condense over time, they jostle in a space that they themselves slowly clear and illuminate. Poets and philosophers can bear the grief of absence by foreseeing, amidst the obscurity of the night, the dawn of the rising day.

20

Potent prophecies of the leap: Marx and Kierkegaard

Philosophy is perhaps the most intimate part of universal history. And without doubt, Hegel interpreted his own philosophy as a final completion, *Vollendung*, a full ending, *volles Ende*, of Western history. Nothing is lost, all is conserved. The ultimate philosophy is the outcome of those that went before it. The World Spirit has reached its destination, consciousness of itself.[1] The system's circle closes, making sure that it has left nothing outside of it. What may come afterward already has the stigma of post-history. The triumphal march of the Absolute Spirit is a narration which – thanks to a well-oiled machine, directed toward substituting external constraints with just as many internal ones – passes from one transcendence to another, from one self-evidence to another, up till the all-concluding conciliation.

But the strenuous effort of the concept, which seeks to harmonise the opposite poles of exteriority and interiority, proves to be in vain. What happens externally, even under the sign of cruelty, oppression, violence, would respond to a form of internal necessity. Conciliation is withered by a deathly breath. The system's circle is destined to explode.

Hegel tried to realise this synthesis between reality and Spirit by walling off the explosive charge latent within his thought and subjecting his system to state power. Was this a victory for philosophy? Or was it not instead a parody of a philosophy which had ended up betraying its own vocation?

What ought to have been the ultimate act of conciliation became the first act of an absolute rupture, an irreparable caesura, which marked the epilogue of the modern age. The reader will recall Hegel's famous sentence, 'What is rational is real, what is real is rational.'[2] It was here that the cracks emerged. Rather than showing themselves thankful and satisfied with the destination that the Spirit's long pilgrimage from Ionia to Jena had now reached – perhaps celebrating it with an interminable feast – Hegel's epigones declared that the idyll had come to an end. What was rational was not yet real; what was real was not yet rational. Though they recognised the 'master's' great merits, in his system they saw the penultimate chapter of history. But precisely for that reason, they had to acknowledge its collapse. The completion of theory had not coincided with its practical realisation, while the individual had been sacrificed on the altar of the universal. Philosophy had to re-begin from here, breaking from the metaphysical schema of completion, to situate itself in a time that knew not of definitive illuminations, a time that was already beyond the proclaimed end of history.

The collapse of the Hegelian system brought about not only a deep crack between above and below, but also a further split between external and internal. The two protagonists of this highly charged caesura were Marx and Kierkegaard, each of them the exponent of one of the two extremes of externality and internality. Hunger and misery, angst and guilt, desperation and death: everything Hegel had imagined could be removed, tempered, harmonised, exploded with disruptive force. Reality was no longer the homeland of reason. And philosophy could not but bear witness to this; better, it could not but unmask it. Should it simply be said that theory was led back to the hive of praxis? That the *bíos theoretikós* was set apart, subjugated, downgraded? And that mobilisation took over from contemplation?

In the final pages of his book *Occidental Eschatology*, published in 1947, Jacob Taubes offered a more complex interpretation of this historic fracture. Taubes chose to conclude on this theme because he was convinced that the epilogue of the Western world introduced a 'new aeon', an enduring epoch of the no-longer and the not-yet.[3] He detected – in particular in the split between external and internal – the temporary capsizing of the revolutionary project, which had been set back by the inability to make the two voices that spoke up in the post-Hegelian period come into harmony in a single conspiracy. With Marx, the dialectic had become externalised to the point of no longer allowing interiority to survive, other than as a fiction; with Kierkegaard, the dialectic had become internalised to the point of cutting off any relations with the world. Hence the extraordinary actuality of this theme.

Taubes provided an original reading of what had happened to philosophy in that decisive moment. At the risk of getting lost, and being defeated anew, philosophy returned to estranging itself into the world in order to denounce its estrangement.[4] It could have wallowed in its now-complete cycle, remaining without-a-world, in a world without philosophy. Or it could have chosen the path of negotiation, stipulating peace agreements in each given situation. This would, in a sense, have sheltered it from the hurricane which followed the fragmentation of a universal system. Instead, it chose tension, and, abandoning any conciliating proposition, simultaneously immersed itself in the world and opposed itself to the world. In so doing, it exposed itself to danger: for the becoming-philosophical of the world is, at once, the becoming-worldly of philosophy. This is an ancient danger, which it would be impossible to skirt around. Yet the estrangement is too acute, too oppressive and painful. The wonder over what could in no way have been self-evident intensified and became exasperated; *páthos* gave way to a passion which, rather than stopping at the concluding cycle, instead concluded that it was time to decide: *aut aut*. On closer inspection, Taubes observed, this was less a decision than a 'leap' – *Sprung*. Philosophy, not only critical but also prophetic, chose the leap of revolution.

Persecuted as heretics, the left-Hegelians were crushed by the university. But perhaps the academy was no longer a refuge for the migrants of thought. Especially in the German context, a separation emerged between philosophy and university life, which climaxed first with Schopenhauer then with Nietzsche. Hunted and pursued by half of Europe's police, Marx fled from one nation to another, finally finding shelter in London where, amidst all manner of difficulties, he wrote *Capital*.

The spark of Hegelian philosophy caught light to the point of becoming a revolutionary blaze. The flame was turned toward the outside world. Indeed, Marx feared what had happened to the Stoics in Antiquity: once the sun sets, thought, just like a moth, is attracted to the lamp of the private. But it was time for dreams, too-long guarded within interiority, finally to be realised. Marx pointed an accusing finger against capitalism, in which the human being was estranged even from its humanity. To denounce this 'world turned upside down' it was necessary to put philosophy back on its feet, after Hegel had made it walk on its head. This did not mean abandoning the terrain of philosophy. Rather, Marx repeatedly confessed that he could not have done without throwing himself into the arms of philosophy once more. The relationship between them was complex and ambivalent. The famous thesis 'The philosophers have hitherto only interpreted the world in various ways; the point is to *change it*' is no exception, in this regard.[5] For while these words are usually read, all too rashly, as an appeal to pragmatism, nothing could have been further from Marx. Bloch observed as much, emphasising that no antithesis exists between interpreting and transforming. Conscious of the emancipatory potential of interpretation and of the practical value of theory, Marx called for a further step toward changing things.[6] Above all, he asked that the 'theoretical spirit' leave the realm of shadows and unleash practical energies. He accorded philosophy a decisive role in emancipation – a role that went beyond the Hegelian dialectic of reason and reality, one that was not only critical but also maieutic. And he wrote: 'The *head* of this emancipation is *philosophy*, its *heart* the *proletariat*. Philosophy cannot realize itself without the transcendence of the proletariat, and the proletariat cannot transcend itself without the realization of philosophy.'[7] This leap into the abyss under the threateningly unchanging sky of history, this utopian passage through which the proletariat would transcend itself, this messianic leap from the realm of necessity to the realm of freedom, could be achieved only thanks to philosophy.

The red thread of the critique of capitalism is alienation. Marx distinguishes between *Entäusserung*, 'estrangement', being outside of one's self, the eccentricity that characterises all that exists, and *Veräusserung*, the profoundly unhuman and anti-human 'alienation' that undermines existence, wounds it in its tension, moreover presenting itself in dissembled form as the self-alienation of the individual. In order to unmask it, it would be necessary to look not at existence in the abstract, but rather at that which lives, or survives, in the capitalist world, where no *communio* arises, where each is isolated and for himself, where freedom is limited to private property, to the right to dispose of one's own resources – regardless of the relation with the other, which, indeed, is nothing but a limit on one's own freedom. Philosophy's gaze concentrates less on politics than on the economy, in order to examine labour close-up – that is, scrutinising the way in which existence realises itself in the capitalist world. Here emerges in all its dark cruelty the alienation that strips the human being – or better, the worker – of the possibility of reconquering himself precisely by estranging himself. What happens in the economic process? The worker can no longer recognise himself in the product of his labour, which is usurped from him by the boss, by the owner of the means of production. Hence why labour is alienated from the worker, or indeed coerced. Only apparently free, the worker is a slave. The fruit of his labour, which has been expropriated from him, has become a 'commodity': something not only estranged from him, but which he must buy back just in order to survive. Marx sheds a light on all this bizarre *quid pro quo*. He does this especially in the first part of his great work *Capital*. Doubtless, the exchanging of commodities is itself something ancient: but in capitalism, all life is determined by the commodity, an enigma rich 'in metaphysical details. Indeed, it has the impalpable and troubling character of a fetish: it is a talisman, a piece of sorcery, which enchants and bewitches. But the divinity worshipped in the world of capital is money. The quintessence of value, money makes all things equivalent by transforming them into commodities. Even including human beings, human existence and human relations. Money inverts, converts and reveals itself to be soul of this subverted world. The ancient *agorá* where citizens meet is now the marketplace where everything is on sale, where the proletarians compelled to give up their labour-power in turn take on the character of commodities.

The proletarian is the human being, lost to himself: his essence is entirely dehumanised, his existence is the complete loss of humanity. For Marx, this is the culmination of alienation, the apogee of capital's infamy. But precisely when the fall into estrangement reaches the deepest abyss, the path of redemption and salvation begins to take form. The protagonist is the proletariat, a 'class with radical chains', a class 'for the dissolution of all classes', which through its 'universal suffering' does not claim any 'particular right'; after all, what is exercised against the proletariat is not a 'particular injustice' but rather 'injustice tout court'.[8] In this alienation the proletariat feels itself reduced to nothing; and in its abjection it makes itself into rebellion, the negative side, the party of revolution, thus capable of breaking the chains of all.

It is not difficult to detect, in this economy of salvation, the messianic character of the proletariat. As Taubes writes, 'Evidently, proletariat does not denote the concrete mass of the proletariat but a historical dialectical entity.'[9] While in this reading the monetary soul has pervaded everything thanks to liberalism's *laissez-faire*, capital capitalises on this by producing a growing mass of the poor and enslaved. Hence the hour has sounded for communism. This means not only the end of private property, but also the onset of an existence which can be articulated on the basis of *Gemeinwesen*, of 'being-in-common'.

The clamour of an apocalyptic catastrophe echoes throughout the analyses of capital. Marx considered such a catastrophe inevitable. In that end-time, nothing could have 'lessen[ed] the birth pangs'.[10] Obsessively following the political happenings in all countries, he never stopped reading them with these same apocalyptic eyes, as he sought to glimpse the ultraviolet of the future that lay therein. First came 1848, then the Paris Commune. And yet, the unreason of history persisted. Thus, this old ultra-modern prophet increasingly withdrew into himself, to discover – ahead of time – the law of history that was meant to lead to the final leap before the realm of freedom.

For Kierkegaard, too, revolutionary humanity is an existence-in-the-leap. But this time it is the individual who makes that leap. What does this have to do with a Dane living in sleepy and provincial Copenhagen, fated to be born at a time when the World Spirit had already concluded its cycle? In this post-history, nothing could be new anymore. The Dane's life would, then, be a footnote, an insignificant codicil; he ought to have recognised that for the World Spirit his life was all in vain.

Kierkegaard's leap is a jump outside of the millennia-long history of Western philosophy. Especially since – as it would seem – that history is already over. It would, then, be necessary to break the luminous thread of concepts. Radical thought does not presume to be a child of its own time, but rather admits its own date of birth.

Guided by infinite doubt – which, unlike Cartesian doubt, does not aim to arrive at certainties – the philosophical gaze no longer allows itself to be enchanted. It denounces the triviality in that which is enlightened, and it seeks out the extraordinary in banality. This would also be the path followed by Walter Benjamin. As confidence evaporated in the centuries-old trick of the self-evident, it is time for the individual to speak; unable to delay any longer, the individual is forced to choose, to take a position: *aut aut*. This is the leap.

Melancholia is Kierkegaard's existential style; it becomes more acute and exasperated by way of an extraneousness to the world, to others, and to himself, which finds no remedy. 'My melancholy is the most faithful mistress I have known; what wonder, then, that I love her in return.'[11] Each of the few episodes that marks his outward existence – including the enigmatic breaking-off of his engagement to Regine Olsen, which appears almost as a literary expedient – only confirms his isolation, distance, marginality. Practising an asceticism that others would find unimaginable, he writes incomprehensible books, throwing himself into unhappiness.

Waiting for Kierkegaard around the corner is derision. The tense, troubled, but also polemical tone of his writings, which contain deep meditation but also irate comments and impassioned invective, draw him a great deal of hostility. Kierkegaard openly attacks the common sense of his contemporaries. And they, in turn, did not spare him offensive critiques and vicious caricatures. He was depicted walking through the streets of Copenhagen dressed in a peculiar garb, his body crippled and warped; he considered himself a martyr of the scorn heaped upon him.

What he does still have is thought. But philosophy cannot be indifferent to existence. Rather, it transforms it; for they who philosophise continually put themselves in the mix.

The individual is no longer the place of doubt; rather, it is the being that doubts itself. Kierkegaard heralds the era in which existence becomes enigmatic to itself.

At the foundation of human existence is angst, the 'mortal illness'. This needs finally to be recognised. This intimate laceration, this deaf desperation, does not sum up Kierkegaard's own personal fate. He sees in angst the fundamental situation of all existence. Who has not felt in their own self that contention between so many threatening possibilities, confronted with which it seems impossible to make any choice? Who has not, therefore, touched their own limit? And yet, this is also where the source of freedom lies – in one's own being-able-to-be. But this, only on condition that angst is accepted and welcomed.

Nonetheless, the choice of a self is not the same thing as becoming ourselves. Rather, this is a matter of putting on one of the many different masks. For each, there is an abyssal distance between one's own interiority and outward existence. But this abyss should finally be explored, in order to bring out the desperation and the discomfort therein.

In his philosophical writings, speaking to himself, Kierkegaard turns to the reader, for whom he sets out an edifying itinerary punctuated by traps, an underground journey made up of galleries and culminating in a ditch. It is as if he wanted to make the reader fall into that desperate obscurity which he was himself so used to inhabiting. A re-evocation of Plato's cave, the ditch is neither dark nor light; rather, it is that internal space where, as the profane light dies away, the eyes can finally begin to see.[12] But the aim is not to arrive at an understanding of immutable forms. And the ditch could perhaps be a castle.

My sorrow is my baronial castle, which lies like an eagle's nest high up on the mountain peak among the clouds. No one can take it by storm. From it I swoop down into actuality and snatch my prey, but I do not stay down there. I bring my booty home, and this booty is a picture I weave into the tapestries at my castle. Then I live as one already dead. Everything I have experienced I immerse in a baptism

of oblivion unto an eternity of recollection. Everything
temporal and fortuitous is forgotten and blotted out. Then
I sit like an old gray-haired man, pensive, and explain the
pictures in a soft voice, almost whispering, and beside me
sits a child, listening, although he remembers everything
before I tell it.[13]

This ditch which Kierkegaard calls a 'castle' so as not
to prompt commiserations from others – a depth which
nonetheless sticks out into the sky, a crystal-clear obscurity
– is the philosopher's abode. It is built of oblivion and
recollection, patterned by images gleaned from reality and
whispered in thoughts to the future child. Such is the verticality of philosophy, which holes itself up or glides down
like a bird.

Nothing is so frightening as to exist, and nor is there anything higher. To transform existence means to bear some
effect on reality. But in the cry of jubilation of his own time,
Kierkegaard perceived all the symptoms of estrangement –
that desolate levelling process where no one embraces their
own angst, no one decides alone anymore, where all discourse has deteriorated into gossip and the common bond
has dissipated amidst the anonymous publicness.

Kierkegaard's choice against his time was his decision
for the individual, redeemed in his infinite difference. He
pointed an accusing finger against the Christianity of his
era, which, he insisted, had deteriorated into a plaything
for the crowd. Thus, this melancholic philosopher recognised himself as an agent of the Almighty, called upon to
remember eternity. And the new era has its beginning in
this memory.

Nonetheless, the reversal of history would not be the
product of a political revolution. There were some points
of convergence with Marx: for Kierkegaard, too, the conceited and corrupt bourgeoisie was guilty, and the arrival
of the Fourth Estate was the event of the epoch. But nothing
could change so long as the human race – at the peak of
estrangement, bled dry by hardships – did not wake up to

interiority and learn to read the infinite concealed within the folds of its own existence.

Powerful prophecies of the leap, both distinguished by an apocalyptic air and an eschatological coloration, Marx and Kierkegaard's philosophies remain divergent and specular. Marx and Kierkegaard are still in exile;[14] with this, Taubes put across the idea that a philosophy responding to the aeon of the no-longer must start again from here.

21

The ecstasy of existence

What about existence in a world without an outside? It is to be assumed that this will have wider repercussions – especially considering that 'existence' means to come outside, to emerge. Existence is intimately linked to philosophy by their common atopic aspect. That is why philosophy must respond to what happens to existence under the ontological regime of the without-an-outside.

Besides, there is no philosophy that is not a philosophy of existence. For all thought starts out from one's own existence – the point of departure for thought and, simultaneously, its point of return. Thus, for philosophy, to take care of existence and of its fate means to recall its own atopia. What would then come to light is the urgency of a radical existentialism.

But would this not be a reckless move – and a blatantly antiquarian one? It seems to detect in the present-day scenario a dominion of ontology over existence, which affirms itself by reducing all that is a 'subject' to the status of an 'object' in the name of the fight against anthropocentrism. One need only mention the now multiple versions of speculative realism.[1] Notwithstanding its interesting cues to reflection, this 'object-oriented ontology' itself seeks an outside, but it does so artificially – beyond time, history and any single existence. Everything exists equally, as each object is made equivalent on the metaphysical plane.[2] This flat ontology, which pursues a mathematical horizontality, ends up reinforcing the saturated immanence and consolidating the exophobic closure. If one starts out from the reality of objects, from their generalised equivalence, the outside is nothing but a mirage and an illusion. Not to mention that in the more or less deliberately programmed oblivion of politics, this equivalence proves to be wholly consonant with capitalism. Rather than speculate on identities starting out from objects, it would instead be necessary to rethink differences. This means choosing the opposite path and thinking existence, in its irreducible eccentricity, before any ontology.

In speaking of 'existentialism', it seems one can never take too many precautions. Already in a 3 March 1947 letter to Elisabeth Blochmann, Heidegger wrote 'I have nothing in common with the smoke clouds of "existentialism".'[3] By this, he sought to distance himself especially from Sartre and French thought. Nonetheless, it cannot be denied that the more or less explicit, more or less openly declared, existentialism that runs through contemporary philosophy ought to be explained also taking into account Heidegger's legacy. And this latter contains more than one ambiguity.

In *Being and Time*, the word 'existence' moves aside in favour of 'being-there'. Dasein thus becomes the new protagonist. There are various factors which dictate such a choice. Heidegger preferred *Dasein* also because he sought to distinguish himself from Jaspers, who was himself delineating a philosophy of *Existenz*. The term which Heidegger chose, already recurrent in the German tradition, moreover has the advantage of referring to Being: being-there is the sole being that has access to Being. And one ought not forget this work's intention, as an exhortation. Heidegger proposes to awaken each single Dasein from its ontic sleep.

Each being-there is always a power-to-be. It should be imagined at a crossroads, faced with the possibilities that open up to it, but which it is on each occasion forced to choose between. On the one hand, it projects itself into the future; on the other, it is 'thrown' in its 'there', in that ineluctably finite condition which it has not chosen. Kierkegaard's suggestions apply here, but so, too, Hölderlin's verses. Heidegger renounces *Existenz* also in order to give greater relief to Dasein in its thrownness, this melancholic orphan consigned to the world in spite of itself. Yet, he also adds a further important reason: namely, in metaphysics, 'existent' has ended up indicating that which is simply present – in short, becoming a synonym for 'real'. But precisely this usage must be avoided, for being-there cannot be assumed statically.[4] Its essence – if one can, indeed, speak of essence – is its existence. Thus, existing ought to be understood in the sense of coming outside, emerging. Being-there emerges from its thrownness, projecting itself beyond. Returning to existence some years later – and there is a famous passage on this in the 'Letter on Humanism' – Heidegger left the 'ecstatic character' in the shadows, and ended up privileging being-there.[5]

Perhaps it is necessary to start out again from this existence, prior to Dasein. At its root, the Latin verb *exsistere* is made up of *ex-*, 'outside', from, and *sistere*, 'to stand, to be positioned, to be situated', deriving from **sta*, 'stand on feet'. Hence the prefix is decisive – it refers to a deviation, a coming-out of stasis. In this is condensed the movement of existence, which surpasses itself in that dynamism which constitutes its power-to-be. Yet, the Latin prefix *ex-* should be distinguished from the Greek *ek-*: the former above all designates exit, the passage from the internal to the external, whereas the latter indicates the ecstatic opening. Heidegger himself sheds light on these two values, which in a sense cross paths in being-there.[6] 'Existence' designates the paradox of 'staying within' even while being ecstatically exposed to the open. Thanks to its original eccentricity, being-there is in the world – it inhabits the world without becoming at one with it. In its stay on earth, it also drags the world into the light – which would not take place without being-there. And this is possible thanks to its incessant ecstatic movement. The inhabitants of the world are, necessarily, eccentric.

Exile, ecstasy, exposition, existence – all that is distinguished by the outside, destined to the beyond, risks succumbing in a globe concentrated and saturated by immanence. A new existentialism would have to refuse any sacrificing of existence in the name of ontology, instead calling being-there back to its singular eccentricity, without which it would be nothing but bare existence. Between ecstasy and bare existence there unfolds that ex-tension which constantly disrupts and interrupts any homogeneous continuity. Such an existentialism would play a decisive political role, blocking all those forms of ontological equivalence produced or supported by the flow of capital. This would mean reviving an existential analytics, evoking the outside, betting on philosophy's exophilosophic vein, and laying claim to an exophilia.

22

For an exophilia

The announcement that the outside had been lost, gone astray, become inaccessible, came already very early, with Zarathustra.[1] For finally, the veil that had hidden the back-world, the world beyond, has fallen; everything is empty, everything is desolate and the same. There is a long path running between this original announcement and Sloterdijk's worried identification of a 'non-round world' which no longer stands opposed to an exteriority. Across this stretch of time, countless voices among sociologists, psychoanalysts, anthropologists, historians, and scholars of literature and the mass media have sounded the alarm over this incessant confusion between the 'within' and the 'outside'. If the private is intimately permeated by the public then, in turn, the public space is nothing but the void of publicness. This has nothing to do with the *pólis*.

Rather, in this half-dreamlike space, troubled by hallucinatory shadows, pervaded by phantasmatic images, where everything *seems* possible and nothing *is* possible, a bare existence survives day by day, cautious and folded in on itself. Its existence is, rather more, a disconsolate in-sistence, which weighs down on its own centre – for it no longer finds a point of access for its own eccentricity.

The other has already been expelled, pushed back, banished. No trace of it is left. What dominates, unchallenged, is an equivalence which encounters no immunitarian defences and – far from the ancient ideal of equality – is itself the product of the monetary soul, of universal exchange, of perpetual calculation. Thanks to this all-pervasive violence, repression mutates into depression. For the self living in the formless space of hypercommunication and hyperconsumption, where distance is abolished by proximity and proximity is patterned by distance, the enemy is an only imaginary figure, for which one can at the very most feel nostalgia. It would at least provide one with an identity. But in the realm of the equivalent, indifference prevails. It is some time since the other lost the aura of the foreigner; now, she is only the immigrant, the refugee, the 'illegal' toward which the angst of one's own existence is directed, in an exophobic imaginary where there is no real fear but rather phobia for the external. The other is only a burden – and, on closer inspection, this means only the burden of one's own existence, reduced to an insistence on the self. The calculations did not work out as planned here: no one had predicted that the negation of the other would also turn out to be a self-negation. Thus, in the zone of well-being surrounded by the gloomy suburbs, the miserable peripheries, the theatres of war, and boundless internment camps for the unwanted, a spiral of self-destructiveness has been set in motion. In this zone of post-immunitarian indifference, of bulimic voracity, of conceitedness, there can be no hospitality. For hospitality is an interruption of the self.

This self has run aground in a riverbed submerged by flows, has become prisoner to the digital network – and it has a difficult time of being itself. This is not the old individualist of the modern era. Rather, it is an ego which has narcissistically sunk into itself, now that its eccentricity has gone astray. The only thing that could save it from this shipwreck is the other – but it slams the door on her. The ego inhabits a sterile resonance chamber, sheltered from any extraneousness, invulnerable to any troubling out-of-placeness. In that digital order where it is befuddled and dazed by information, it has gone blind and deaf. While imagination has declined, thinking, which is always thinking of the beyond and of the other, has been reduced to repeated calculation. Here, there are no events that could interrupt this perverse and unbearable routine; and even if there were, they would go unnoticed. Just as a friend's voice would go unheard.

Where the ecstasy of existence is missing, where eccentricity vanishes, the passage that leads outside is blocked off, the path toward the other is obstructed, and a prohibition raised against co-existence, that common wakefulness that founds and safeguards the city. Without *philía* there is no *pólis*. Plato and Aristotle were well aware of this. Hence the task of philosophy, which has its only *ubi consistam* in *phileîn*: the task of restoring wonder, provoking disconcertment, arousing strangeness, and instilling passion for the other.

23

The philosophy of awakening

Time, then, for philosophers to return to the city? But how could atopia be preserved? An esoteric author, an anarchic communist, an obsessive collector, a freelance journalist, a chaotic intellectual, Walter Benjamin opens up a new passageway. But while he offered precious insights, few have been able to grasp them – even among his followers, who have often ended up putting him on a pedestal.

Benjamin ventures out into the metropolitan city, travels down its tree-lined boulevards, its labyrinthine alleyways, ends up in its one-way streets. But most importantly, he penetrates into its inner passageways, its commercial arcades, which are temples of capital, the homeland of commodities, 'the dream houses of the collective'.[1] These magically illuminated corridors of glass, marble and steel, with their many boutiques and shops brimming with fashionable objects, are enchanted places, 'fairy-tale castles'. Among the games of mirrors, the perceptual surprises and the *trompes-l'œil*, these marvellous illusions are monuments to progress, the sites where the phantasmagoria of modernity are celebrated. More than summing up an epoch, a 'lapse of time', a *Zeitraum*, they represent the

Zeit-traum, the 'time of dreams' of advanced capitalism. It is, therefore, decisively important to enter into this miniature world of mirrors, private and closed, an exclusive space of exclusion, the magical landscape of a dream that numbs, makes us sleep, turns us into sleepwalkers. Its optical tricks are so many dreamlike illusions.

'Capitalism was a natural phenomenon with which a new dream-filled sleep came over Europe, and through it, a reactivation of mythic forces.'[2] For the critical theorist, this turns out to be an eminently political endeavour. It is not enough to explore the contemporary city, letting oneself be carried away by estrangement, to lose oneself in erotic adventures and perturbing experiences, to intoxicate oneself amidst marginal encounters and occult premonitions. This was the original choice of the surrealists, from Louis Aragon to André Breton. Yet, whereas they linger in this seductive kingdom of dreams, Benjamin follows them only up to a certain point, before then distancing himself. Beyond travelling through the labyrinth of the city, projecting the light of a profane enlightenment, much more was necessary – an explosive moment, almost as if throwing a bomb, to wake up the dreaming collective, to set the sleeping modernity back with its feet on the ground.

Here re-emerges the philosopher as guardian of the *pólis*. Surprised and worried, he denounces the 'dream of the time' which sends the city to sleep in the middle of the day, risking its ruin and dissolution. Does this mean to point out a threat, to issue a warning? These mythological forces, too violent in their ambiguous seductive power, these phantasmagoria, are too powerful. The philosopher comes back into the city in order to interrupt a state of apparent wakefulness which in fact conceals a catastrophic sleepwalking. He does not limit himself to cognition and recognition; for he issues a call to action. In the age of the capitalist dream, philosophy orients itself toward a new 'constellation of awakening'.[3]

But what is 'awakening'? A sort of rite of passage, the experience of crossing a threshold. Proust immortalised

this moment in the morning half-sleep, in which consciousness returns to itself, orienting itself in the world. Yet this
goes not only for the life of the individual, but also for
that of the collective. In such a case, awakening sets the
pace of history, beats its rhythm. The dreaming collective
does not know history, and lives in a flux which, though
perceived as an ever-new, is in fact an always-the-same.
This is the place where the enigma of modernity, the recent
version of the eternal return, should be deciphered. Hence
why Benjamin writes 'ringen um das Erwachen aus dem
Kollektivraum' – 'struggle to awake from the collective
dream'.[4]

However fleeting and unstable the limit between sleep
and wakefulness may be, it cannot disappear. The danger
is that of consigning oneself to a dreamlike universe, wallowing in dreams. But the awakening is not that produced
by Reason – an accomplice of the virulent myth of progress. It is better to put down this 'whetted axe' and trust
rather more in 'cunning', a dialectic able to overturn the
fairy-tale world of capitalism.[5]

The awakening does not erase the dream; rather, it introduces a new relationship. This owes to the similarity which
links awakening to memory, *Erwachen* and *Erinnerung*.
The experience of awakening is the entry into the suspended
time between sleep and wakefulness, an inarticulable synthesis which marks a point of rupture, when everything
appears in its surrealistic expression. Thus, in half-sleep
– in that not-yet-conscious-knowledge – the memory of
that which is closest, most banal, most within reach, is
suddenly turned on. This is not a matter of dreaming while
awake, but of waking up to the dream. For the dream can
only be remembered once one has woken up. 'Carry out
what has been in remembering of the dream!'[6]

Although Benjamin repeatedly returns to compare the
individual with the collective, he does not look to the
natural alternation of sleep and wakefulness, but rather
to the historical event that is awakening. It is here, on this
threshold, that the philosopher situates himself. Doubtless,

his place is not ever so distant from that of the historian who, taking his leave from the old historiographical schemas and the ossified 'once upon a time' is prepared to interpret the dreams of the past.

But the philosopher, who has a child's eyes and recognises the new where adults are unable to do so, sees that this awakening needs to be helped along. Benjamin speaks, rather, of a 'technology of awakening'. By this he means the 'dialectical . . . turn of remembrance'.[7] The philosopher acts in the present, which he reads not in a historical way but rather in a 'political' one, in order to light the fuse of an explosive that had already been set in the past.

The break from the realm of dreams, the awakening from the deep sleep of the collective consciousness, does not come about through the brute violence of a weapon. What is required, rather, are the abilities and dexterity to carry out pyrotechnic exercises which, unexpected and surprising, clear the path, lighting up here and there that which is secretly waiting to catch light. The path that Benjamin chooses, as he ventures out into the *passages* of Paris, responds to a complex kinetics which is simultaneously both horizontal and vertical. The city is like consciousness, individual and collective. By day, during wakefulness, one passes from one street to another, turning past one corner and the next almost oblivious; by night, one turns back to those hidden points from which one descends into the underground through dark tunnels. The image evokes the Heraclitean *pólis* with its basis in the night-time. But here, the philosopher does not stop at issuing a warning to his fellow citizens; rather, he himself heads down below. He heads down into the *métro,* among the gods of the sewers and the fairies of the catacombs, into openings, where rather than a Theban virgin being thrown each year, each day thousands of workers are sacrificed. He does not purport to invert time – who could? – but rather to remember dreams, the dreams of past generations, whose traces remain in the city. A psychoanalyst of the collective consciousness, the philosopher makes his way through the *passages* in order to relive those dreams, summon them back into memory. He does so in order that those who have dreamed have not done so in vain, and that those who now dream can re-dream those dreams without being taken away by the torpor thus induced. 'Arcades are houses or passages having no outside – like the dream.'[8] The philosopher does not shy from the fact that his journey is also spectral, for travelling far and wide he may also be followed by troubled shadows, unredeemed souls, phantasms of defeat. Derrida dwelled on these spectral spaces at length.

But what is the meaning of a dialectic which adopts dreamlike themes right upon the moment of awakening? If he cannot guess at the future, the philosopher is a prophet of the past. And here lies that which Benjamin calls the 'Copernican revolution in the vision of history': the past is not a fixed point, as if it were a closed and concluded era which the present would have to approach asymptotically. This historicist conception, which boasts of recounting 'the facts' as they really took place, has contributed to the narcosis. It is necessary to reverse this and say that the past is constantly reconfigured as it bursts into the present. It has a posthumous life; indeed, this is the forefront of the struggle. 'Politics achieves primacy over history.' One can provoke, or better evoke – almost with an involuntary memory – a synergy of times in which past and present illuminate one another, like a bolt of lightning shedding light on the future. It is a uchronic alliance which, in its eccentricity, makes no mystery of its will to confront Zarathustra, put a stop to repetition, suspend the eternal return of sameness. It seeks to interrupt the immemorial night of times in order to arrest that *perpetuum mobile* and the use made of it by the capitalism of time, whose clairvoyance is but a police-like prevention of the future.

What is needed is not invention, but inventiveness. And, doubtless, also a plan. Benjamin offers an extraordinary proof of this in his *Denkbilder*, 'images of thought', miniature composites of carefully gathered and juxtaposed

parts, montages in which forgotten fragments, kaleido-
scopic representations of the metropolis, its triumphs and
its ruins, find new life. The philosopher is a collector. He
shakes up kitsch and calls for a collection to be made.
His actions, his gestures, are political. The collection, this
'opposite of utility', is eminently philosophical. Thus, the
collector unbinds the object from the ties that linked it
to the magic circle in which it was fixed, and introduces
it into a new historical order. Everything which has been
thought, remembered, becomes the treasure chest, the
frame, of her practical memory. Benjamin writes, 'It must
not be assumed that the collector, in particular, would
find anything strange in the *topos hyperouranios* – that
place beyond the heavens which, for Plato, shelters the
unchangeable archetypes of things.'⁹ To bring the hyperuranic among the crowd, into the bazaars, the markets, the
deafening tract – to capture snapshots of tramps, beggars,
bums, to bring them to the hyperuranial. Such are the new
tasks of a subversive philosophy ready to immerse itself
in the phantasmagorical belly of the metropolis – that is,
the homeland of consumption, the temple of capital. Put
on display in the windows of the *grands magasins* and
the boutiques, commodities are the celebrated object of
worship. The traces of labour and exploitation have been
carefully erased, and all that does come across is their
seductive, impudent sparkle. Yet, for Benjamin, commodities are not only fetishes, an index of suffering, a sign
of false consciousness, as Marx thought. They are also
images of desire, for they harbour hidden promises, aspi-
rations, utopian impulses, which ought to be unveiled and
redeemed. Hence, critique is not enough to implode the
capitalist phantasmagoria; there also needs to be an awakening from sleep, the dialectical speculativity which reflects
a beyond, the redemption of posthumous life.

24

Fallen angels and rag-pickers

Mindful of his ancient defeat, the philosopher enters back into the *pólis*, which in the meantime has become a global metropolis. He does so in order to shed light on its twilight, to illuminate its ruin. There is no attempt, here, to overcome the fracture, which remains irreparable. Far from the protection of the academy, the internal emigration becomes itinerant exile, vagabondage, lostness, distraction – but also an anarchist rereading of the architectures of the *pólis*. Philosophy returns, defeated, to seal an alliance with the defeated.

No philosopher-king, no sovereignty. That melancholic extraterrestrial wanders around the city like a fallen angel. He brings his precious saturnine gaze into the urban turmoil. He makes no claim to be watching from up on high, to raise himself up above. He does not consider himself a privileged spectator – rather, he is mixed in among the crowd; he has no bird's-eye view. But he still has his wings – however broken they are – and the memory of a dream of justice. Politically, he is an asylum-seeker in his own city. In this non-belonging, this non-citizenship, he finds himself together with many foreigners, exiles, refugees, immigrants, shoulder to shoulder with the victims of overbearing financial wealth, among the beggars and gamblers, the hawkers and the nomads, the unemployed and the desperate, the residue of the 'world of dreams' that has produced horrendous nightmares.

In the Berlin which he was readying to leave forever, his Berlin, to which he was linked by an enigmatic affinity and by childhood memories, Benjamin was the exile traveller, the *flâneur* in search of a return, amidst the urgent need to depart. He thus showed how philosophy can maintain its atopic trait even as it criss-crosses the city, everywhere inscribing the atopia of another city as it passes through the galleries and alleyways, the parks and basements. The philosopher thus disfigures, overthrows, sets off fuses. He excavates and recalls – he recalls and excavates. He goes along deciphering a secret counter-history hidden behind the facades. He recovers that which is supposedly banal, ridiculous, disdained, condemned to obsolescence. He salvages the tradition of the oppressed, redeems the memory of the dead. And he achieves some little victories.

An eccentric inhabitant conscious of his extraneousness, he takes up residence among the homeless, the trampled upon, the lowliest, and makes common cause with the alienated. He could be their storyteller. He never tires of speaking of the outside, of pointing to the beyond. But he is running out of breath and catastrophe is imminent. He may well *aspire*, but he will never manage to *conspire*.

The image of Socrates in the market square in dialogue with his fellow citizens has gone all blurry, become irreparably distant. This also owes to the reality that few people focus on words, and language has been debased. Philosophy remains a killjoy – and more than ever, it is out-of-place. Benjamin imagines it as a 'rag-picker', a *Lumpensammler*. At daybreak he gathers up rags of speech, scraps of language, tossing them into his cart; a little drunk, he grumbles and growls. But not without letting these faded cotton remnants – 'humanity', 'inwardness', 'absorption' – flutter derisively in the morning wind. A philosopher in the city can be a 'rag-picker at the first light of day – at the dawn of the revolution'.[1]

Benjamin speaks of the revolution in many different ways, yet also cautiously: he talks of an emergency brake, an interruption, a leap. For his gaze pushes toward the end. An outsider also within the Left, Benjamin was not so far from the 'anarchist opposition'. It is thus worth remembering his words: 'Ethics, applied to history, is the doctrine of revolution, applied to the state, the doctrine of anarchy.'[2]

25

Anarchist postscript

As inhabitants of a paradoxical 'territory', philosophers have to be careful not to stop intervening in the world. But nor can they forget the disasters which have resulted from the political territorialisations of philosophical atopia. Precisely because the *pólis* requires philosophy's transversal gaze, philosophy must remain unconditional in its relationship with the world.

This means preserving the alpha privative which is at the foundation of philosophy – and not denying this negativist trait. Articulated already in Socratic non-knowledge, this latter removes any beginning, thus allowing for philosophy's internal tension, its splitting *in actu*. Its *arché* is always an-archic. At the very foundation of philosophy is a close bond which links atopia, uchronia and anarchy. The out-of-place is a counter-time that undermines any principle, deposes any command. Not only does philosophy not fall within the order of the *arché*, but it delegitimises and subverts any such order. In this sense, both the warning philosophy issues and its promise are condensed within the alpha privative.

The question of philosophical an-archy is eminently

theoretical, before it is political. Beyond touching on the theme of the ultimate foundation, it revolves around sovereignty. A philosophy which, already starting in the twentieth century, distanced itself from any foundational proposal, emphasising the distinction between itself and the sciences, and resuming the Greek tradition, cannot but interrogate the *arché*. It is no accident that, in such a context, the subject is itself deconstructed. This happens already in *Being and Time*, when Heidegger unleashes an unprecedented attack against the supposed autonomy of the subject.[1] As the deconstruction proceeds, it becomes sharper, scrutinising this famous protagonist of philosophical discourse top to bottom to discover that it is far from transparent in its self-consciousness. Rather, the subject represents an indecipherable enigma, even to its own eyes; for an other resides in its self, and its ideas and its actions are heteronomous. Free will, the linchpin of liberalism, that idea of liberty based on property, gives way to a self which allows for not only expropriation but also for heteroaffectivity and vulnerability.[2] Destabilised by the other, the self then interrogates itself on this dependency.

Levinas in particular put the autonomous subject under scrutiny, subjecting it to a sharp and severe critique. He bluntly denounced its violent aspect, its repetitive subjugating action, its will to swallow up the other to the point of annihilating it. Incapable of leaving itself, and folded in on its own ego, this autarchic subject has purported to be the legislator for both itself and the universe. Concerned only by its own sovereignty, yearning to assert its emphatic identity, to intimate and to impose its conceited priority, this detestable self, posing itself as its own origin and principle, holds itself to be absolute, let loose, unbound from any responsibility. The crimes of the last century weighed on his conscience. Levinas thus addressed his charge-sheet against that modern philosophy which celebrated the epic of the sovereign subject that self-poses and self-governs.

Seeking to debunk this myth – which is still stubbornly influential in ethics as in politics – Levinas suggested an inversion, or better, a subversion of the self's relation to the other.[3] He did this by taking away the *arché* of priority which the self had so despotically arrogated to itself. Before the self, in an immemorial past, there was always-already the other that convokes the self, interrogates it, to which it is called to respond. This is not the product of some act of voluntary adherence – that is, some evaluation of whether to say yes or no. Rather, it comes simply from the unfolding of the self – without any possibility of choice, without conditions. For the self can exist only in that unfolding, in that incessant exodus. Before the self comes the other. Before freedom comes responsibility. And this latter, being without either a principle or a command, is an anarchic responsibility.

In pointing an accusing finger against the autarchy of the subject, Levinas brings up a wider question which his writing addresses only in part, perhaps on account of the primacy attributed to ethics, relegating politics onto a secondary plane. Thus, it is not possible to follow him beyond, along this path.

For certain, a philosophy that wishes to free itself from the alpha privative – something which has cut through and coloured it from the outset – has sought to build itself on archic foundations, however tacitly. For this very reason, the theme of archic sovereignty extends well beyond ethics and, indeed, has its clearest and most enduring effects on politics. From Plato to Schmitt via Hobbes, traditional political thought is obsessed by the archic act – foundation, institution, declaration – which inaugurates the sovereign subject capable of governing. It is not difficult to make out how the sovereignty of the individual corresponds, in the government of the many, to the sovereignty of the state. The archic-ness of politics – not to speak of archi-economy – remains dominant.

If perhaps the moment has shed light on these archic foundations, then the path opened up by Levinas may prove to be a valuable one. He was followed by Abensour, in the essay 'An-Archy Between Metapolitics and Politics', first appearing in 2002 and then republished in the multiauthor volume *The Anarchist Turn* in 2013.[4] In the pages which Levinas dedicates to 'anarchy', the word – often hyphenated – has an ethical value and regards the 'intrigue' of the subject, her anarchic responsibility. Yet it is clear that what is being examined here is the philosophical *arché*, understood as both principle and command. Thus two meanings come to light: on the one hand, an-archy is that which comes before, which precedes any principle; on the other, it is that which remains to contradict and challenge an instituted principle.[5] In the first case, its value is 'pre-political' or 'anti-political', whereas in the second it is manifestly political. Levinas thus himself reattaches an-archy to anarchism. Anarchy: 'that which contests the omnipotence of the state'.[6] Concerned not to make anarchy slip into mere confusion, as many would, Levinas specifies that an-archy is 'disorder' only insofar as it is a 'different order'. In this sense it 'stops the ontological game'. Hence the irreducibility of anarchy which, refusing synthesis, in its radical 'negation' prevents the state erecting itself in the guise of All. But Levinas also adds a provocative line, which he repeats twice over: 'an-archy does not reign', 'anarchy cannot be sovereign, like an *arché*'.[7] If it must be a political form – as anarchism understands it – then the question of sovereignty is posed.

Schürmann also got to grips with the theme of *arché* in his now-famous book *Heidegger on Being and Acting: From Principles to Anarchy*. He makes a complex attempt to deconstruct the archic structure, rereading not only the critique of metaphysics but Heidegger's entire philosophy according to the 'principle of anarchy'. As he describes the paradoxically contradictory character of this new principle of the non-principle, which liberates action from any *arché*, Schürmann particularly aims to separate origin and command. He does so in order to allow the flourishing of a non-archic origin, an origin that does not command, which is thus able to resituate the 'Heideggerian enterprise' by unbinding it from any foundation and, most importantly, from any command.[8] In short, as Agamben has suggested, this would mean a 'democratic reading of Heidegger'.[9] For his part, already in the first pages Schürmann makes clear that he is not using 'anarchy' in the sense of Proudhon, Bakunin and classical anarchism: 'What these masters sought was to *displace* the origin, to substitute the "rational" power, *principium*, for the power of authority, *princeps* – as metaphysical an operation as there has been.'[10]

However different their contexts and their aims, the same critique is echoed in both Levinas and Schürmann: classical anarchism is metaphysical. It has replaced one *arché* with another – it has not considered sovereignty. When confronted in theoretical terms, the question of an-archy thus has inevitable political implications. Abensour prefers the expression 'metapolitical', by this meaning not a politics that comes after ethics – as per Levinas – still less one that comes on top of it, which looks down from on high. Rather, he means a politics that points beyond the political order. This is also how Critchley conceives it, speaking of a 'metapolitical disturbance'.[11]

A philosophy intent on preserving the alpha privative – keeping it as its own foundation – is an an-archist philosophy. In a political perspective, closely connected with the theoretical one, this makes it necessary once again to turn the gaze to the outside, in this case, beyond the state, putting sovereignty in question.

The political 'outside' is constantly evaded, denied, rejected. This, not only by a *pólis* which wants to immunise itself by erecting high walls, but also by those philosophical currents which provide their own endorsement to immunisation, celebrate the saturated immanence, tighten the borders. If it appears impossible to think beyond state borders and press on beyond sovereignty, this is because the state-centric order of the globe is uncritically assumed as a natural rather than historical fact.[12] This model of state sovereignty has been the epicentre of politics for centuries: it draws its map and traces its limits. Thus the internal sphere subjected to sovereign power is separated from the external one, consigned to anarchy.

Rather than indicating that which comes before any principle, or that which contradicts and disturbs the instituted principle – in a pre-political, anti-political or meta-political sense – the word 'anarchy' ends up meaning disorder *qua* absence of government, thus assuming a merely pejorative sense. This legitimises state sovereignty as the only condition of order, the sole alternative to the absence of government. Anarchy becomes another way of indicating the confusion that rages in the unlimited outside.

At work, here, is the well-fated narration provided by Hobbes. He holds that sovereign power is instituted in order to overcome the chaos of nature, from which civil conflict could always spring; and that it is also the fruit of a commonly agreed pact. Hobbes goes so far as to make the state a 'person', an almost anthropomorphic figure, to whose internal sovereignty there corresponds an external sovereignty held in check by the other states. With a move that was destined to have enduring effects, he projected the Leviathan – chosen as the emblem of sovereign power – beyond the borders. The savage lawlessness contained internally reproduces itself in international relations, where war can break out between the wolf-like states.

The dichotomy between internal and external, sovereignty and anarchy, cuts through all modern thought. Reaching our own time, it imposes a hierarchy of problems, prescribes solutions, justifies principles. It is a constitutive dichotomy, for it delineates also the limits of political philosophy, which in large part adapts itself to the presupposition of sovereign statehood. It goes without saying that this introduces value judgements. On the one hand there is the internal space, with the prospect of living well, with the victory of progress and all its consequences and successes, amidst justice, democracy and human rights. On the other there is the external space, in which there is, at the very most, survival, where all that seems possible are vague cosmopolitan projects for a confederation of peoples, if not the re-proposition of a global state. Globalisation does change the scenario but does not really undermine the dichotomy between sovereignty and anarchy. Nonetheless, the outlook is widened, exposing the limits of a politics anchored within traditional borders, unable to turn its gaze toward the landscape outside, beyond the barriers of sovereignty.

The archic act that guides a politics reduced to police-style governance, oriented toward the depoliticisation of the world, can be thwarted by an anarchy which, maintaining its own pre-political, anti-political and meta-political value, is a disturbance to order. This demands a critical embrace of classical anarchism – critical because, anchored in metaphysics, it ends up constituting itself as a principle, reproposing the archic sovereignty which it should instead challenge. The accent on liberty is a proof of this, an attestation that its protagonist is the autonomous and autarchic subject. Yet, the task at hand is to articulate another anarchism, starting out from the multiple and different forms that anarchy is taking on in the contemporary scenario. In an era in which the state, faced with the undermining of its sovereignty, seeks to control and saturate all political space, it is necessary to turn the gaze not only outside its borders but also within its territory, in the interstitial times and spaces which are opening up. Politics is a demand for justice – and what thus needs articulating is an anarchism of responsibility.

Notes

1 The saturated immanence of the world

1 Peter Sloterdijk, *Globes. Spheres Volume II: Macrospherology*, New York: semiotext(e), 2014.
2 Hartmut Rosa, *Alienation and Acceleration: Towards a Critical Theory of Late Modern Temporality*, Aarhus: NSU Press, 2010.
3 Roberto Esposito, *Immunitas: The Protection and Negation of Life*, Cambridge: Polity Press, 2013.
4 Frédéric Neyrat, *Atopias: Manifesto for a Radical Existentialism*, New York: Fordham University Press, 2018.
5 Michael Hardt and Antonio Negri, *Empire*, Cambridge, MA: Harvard University Press, 2000.
6 Déborah Danowski and Eduardo Batalha Viveiros de Castro, *The Ends of the World*, Cambridge: Polity, 2017.
7 Isabelle Stengers, *Au temps des catastrophes. Résister la barbarie qui vient*, Paris: La Découverte, 2013.
8 Slavoj Žižek, *Demanding the Impossible*, Cambridge: Polity, 2013.
9 For accelerationist positions, see, for instance Benjamin Noys, *Malign Velocities: Acceleration and Capitalism*, Winchester: Zero Books, 2014.
10 Mark Fisher, *Capitalist Realism: Is There No Alternative?*, Winchester: Zero Books, 2010.

2 Heraclitus, wakefulness and the original communism

1 Diogenes Laërtius, *The Lives and Opinions of Eminent Philosophers*, London: G. Bell and Sons, 1915, p. 376.
2 G.W.F. Hegel, *Lectures on the History of Philosophy*, D, text from marxists.org.
3 See fragments B 1, B 26, B 73, B 75, B 87 and B 89. On this theme, see Martin Buber's original essay 'Dem Gemeinschaftlichen folgen' (1956), in *Logos. Zwei Reden*, Heidelberg: Lambert Schneider, 1962, pp. 31–72; see also Peter Sloterdijk, *Weltfremdheit*, Frankfurt: Suhrkamp, 1993, pp. 344 et sqq.

3 The narcosis of light: on the night of capital

1 Novalis, 'Hymnen an die Nacht' (1800), in *Werke*, ed. G. Schulz, Munich: C.H. Beck, 1969, p. 41.
2 Jonathan Crary, *24/7: Late Capitalism and the Ends of Sleep*, London: Verso, 2014.
3 Maurice Blanchot, *The Writing of the Disaster*, Lincoln: University of Nebraska Press, 2015.
4 Emmanuel Levinas, *Existence and Existents*, The Hague: Nijhoff, 1978; *Otherwise than Being, or Beyond Essence*, Boston: Dordrecht, 1991.

5 Wonder – a troubled passion

1 See Plato, *Lysis* 218a-b; *Symposium*, 204a; *Phaedrus*, 278d.
2 In Thomas Hobbes's translation.
3 See Plato, *Theaetetus*, 155d; Aristotle, *Metaphysics*, 980a 21–982a 3. On this theme, see Jeanne Hersch, *L'étonnement philosophique: une histoire de la philosophie*, Paris: Gallimard, 2017.

6 Between heavens and abysses

1 *Theaetetus*, 174a, trans. Harold Fowler.
2 Hans Blumenberg, *The Laughter of the Thracian Woman*, London: Bloomsbury, 2015.
3 *Politics*, 1259a 5–8, trans. H. Rackham.

7 Socrates' atopia

1 See Plato, *Symposium*, 215a, 221d; *Alcibiades*, 106a; *Theaetetus*, 149a; *Gorgias*, 494d.
2 See Plato, *Phaedrus*, 251d; *Symposium*, 215a.
3 See Plato, *Meno*, 80a; *Symposium*, 217e, 218b; *Apology*, 30e.
4 Gernot Böhme, *Der Typ Sokrates*, Frankfurt: Suhrkamp, 2002.
5 On the sources and Socrates' thought, see Heinrich Maier, *Sokrates, sein Werk und seine geschichtliche Stellung*, Darmstadt: Scienta Uerlag Aalen, 1964.
6 Gregory Vlastos, *Socrates: Ironist and Moral Philosopher*, Ithaca: Cornell University Press, 1992, pp. 47–9.
7 Jacques Derrida, *La carte postale: de Socrate à Freud at au-delà*, Paris: Flammarion, 1980.
8 See the *Symposium*, 220a–c, trans. Harold Fowler.
9 *First Alcibiades*, 106a, trans. W.R.M. Lamb.
10 On this term, see Michel Foucault, 'Of Other Spaces: Utopias and Heterotopias', in *Rethinking Architecture: A Reader in Cultural Theory*, ed. Neil Leach, New York: Routledge, 1997, pp. 330–6.

8 A political death

1 *Phaedrus*, 230c, trans. Harold Fowler.
2 *Phaedo*, 96a-99d, trans. W.R.M. Lamb.
3 *Apology*, 23b, trans. W.R.M. Lamb.
4 See also *Symposium*, 215e-216c; *Charmides*, 165e-167a.
5 On this, see Aldo Brancacci, 'Socrate e il tema semantico della coscienza', in Gabriele Giannantoni and Michel Narcy (eds.), *Lezioni socratiche*, Naples: Bibliopolis, 1997, pp. 281–301.
6 *Meno*, 79e-80a, trans. W.R.M. Lamb.
7 See Hannah Arendt, *Socrate*, Milan: Cortina, 2015.
8 Leo Strauss, *Jerusalem and Athens: Some Preliminary Reflections*, New York: City College, 1967.
9 For a reconstruction of this history, see Maria Michela Sassi, *Indagine su Socrate. Persona, cittadino, filosofo*, Turin: Einaudi, 2015.
10 Maurice Merleau-Ponty, *Éloge de la philosophie*, Paris: Gallimard, 1953, p. 53.
11 Cicero, *Tusculan Disputations*, I, 30, trans. J.E. King; Michel de Montaigne, *Essays of Montaigne*, vol. 1, trans. Charles Cotton, New York: Edwin C. Hill, 1910, p. 179.

12 Rainer Maria Rilke, *Duino Elegies*, London: Hogarth Press, 1939.
13 *Phaedo*, 67d-e, trans. W.R.M. Lamb.
14 Martin Heidegger, *Being and Time*, Oxford: Blackwell, 1962.
15 Hans-Georg Gadamer, 'The Proofs of Immortality in Plato's Phaedo', in *Dialogue and Dialectic: Eight Hermeneutical Studies on Plato*, New Haven: Yale University Press, 1980, pp. 21–38.
16 Friedrich Nietzsche, *The Gay Science. With a Prelude in Rhymes and an Appendix of Songs*, New York: Vintage Books, 1974, p. 274.

9 Plato – when philosophy headed into exile within the city

1 Peter Sloterdijk, 'The City and its Negation: An Outline of Negative Political Theory', in *The Aesthetic Imperative: Writings on Art*, New York: John Wiley & Sons, 2017.

10 Migrants of thought

1 Diogenes Laërtius, *The Lives and Opinions of Eminent Philosophers*, VI, 63.
2 Novalis, 'Aus dem "Allgemeinen Brouillon"', *Werke*, ed. Gerhard Schulz, Munich: C.H. Beck, 1987, p. 491.
3 Martin Heidegger, *The Fundamental Concepts of Metaphysics: World, Finitude, Solitude*, Bloomington: Indiana University Press, 1995, pp. 5–8.
4 See Plato, *Phaedrus*, 249c-d; see also *Republic*, 517a, *Theaetetus*, 172c.
5 Hannah Arendt, *The Life of the Mind*, Boston: Harcourt, 1981, p. 197 et sqq.
6 Ibid., p. 200.
7 Ludwig Wittgenstein, *The Big Typescript*, Vienna: Springer, 2000.
8 Arendt, *The Life of the Mind*, p. 199.
9 Peter Sloterdijk, *Scheintod im Denken: von Philosophie und Wissenschaft als Übung*, Berlin: Suhrkamp, 2012.

11 'What is philosophy?'

1 Hermann Lübbe (ed.), *Wozu Philosophie? Stellungnahmen eines Arbeitskreises*, Berlin: De Gruyter, 2014.

2 G.W.F. Hegel, *Elements of the Philosophy of Right*, trans. H.B. Nisbet, Cambridge: Cambridge University Press, 1991, p. 21.
3 Martin Heidegger, *What is That – Philosophy?*, trans. Eva T.H. Brann, Annapolis: St. John's College, 1991, p. 4.
4 Ibid., p. 10.
5 Ibid., p. 25.
6 Martin Heidegger, *The End of Philosophy*, Chicago: University of Chicago Press, 2003.
7 Immanuel Kant, *Prolegomena to Any Future Metaphysics*, trans. Jonathan Bennett, Introduction, 22, https://www.early-moderntexts.com/assets/pdfs/kant1783.pdf.
8 Heidegger, *Fundamental Concepts of Metaphysics*, p. 4.
9 Ibid., p. 22.

12 Radical questions

1 Immanuel Kant, *Critique of Pure Reason*, New York: Macmillan, 1922.
2 Martin Heidegger, *The Question Concerning Technology and Other Essays*, New York: Garland, 1977, p. 35.

13 The out-of-place of metaphysics

1 Martin Heidegger, 'Phänomenologische Interpretation zu Aristoteles' (1921–22), in Id., *GA*, LXII, 2: *Phänomenologische Interpretation zu Aristoteles – Einführung in die phänomenologische Forschung*, ed. W. Bröcker and K. Bröcker-Oltmanns, Frankfurt: Klostermann 2005, p. 11; see also *Kant and the Problem of Metaphysics*, Bloomington: Indiana University Press 1997.
2 Ernst Bloch, 'Tübinger Einleitung in die Philosophie' (1963), in *Werkausgabe*, XIII, Frankfurt: Suhrkamp, 1963, pp. 354 et sqq.

14 Dissent and critique

1 Gilles Deleuze and Félix Guattari, *What is Philosophy?*, New York: Columbia University Press, 1994, p. 5; Friedrich Nietzsche, 'On Truth and Lies in a Nonmoral Sense', in *The Portable Nietzsche*, New York: Viking Press, 1976, p. 46.
2 Karl Jaspers, *Von der Wahrheit. Philosophische Logik*, Munich: R. Piper Verlag, 1947, pp. 285 and 465.

3 As is clear from Albertus Magnus's *Summa Theologiae*.
4 See Max Horkheimer, 'The Social Function of Philosophy', *Radical Philosophy* 3:10, 1972, pp. 10–14. See also Theodor W. Adorno, *Philosophische Terminologie*, Frankfurt: Suhrkamp, 1973.

15 The twentieth century: breaks and traumas

1 For a panoramic view, see Remo Bodei, *La filosofia nel Novecento (e oltre)*, Milan: Feltrinelli, 2015.
2 Jürgen Habermas, 'Does Philosophy Still Have a Purpose' (1971), in *Philosophical-Political Profiles*, Cambridge: Polity Press, 2012, p. 4.
3 Peter Sloterdijk, *What Happened in the Twentieth Century? Towards a Critique of Extremist Reason*, Cambridge: Polity Press, 2018.
4 Eric Hobsbawm, *Age of Extremes: The Short Twentieth Century, 1914–1991*, New York: Viking, 1994.
5 Alain Badiou, *The Century*, Cambridge: Polity Press, 2018.

16 After Heidegger

1 I refer the reader to my *Heidegger, the Jews, and the Shoah*, Cambridge: Polity Press, 2017, and *Heidegger and the Jews: The Black Notebooks*, Cambridge: Polity Press, 2018.
2 Hans Blumenberg, *Die Verführbarkeit des Philosophen*, ed. Manfred Sommer in collaboration with the Hans Blumenberg-Archiv, Frankfurt: Suhrkamp, 2000, especially pp. 100–6.
3 Hannah Arendt, 'Martin Heidegger at Eighty', *New York Review of Books*, 21 October 1971, pp. 50–4.
4 Hans-Georg Gadamer, 'Back from Syracuse?', *Critical Inquiry* 15:2, 1989, pp. 427–30.
5 Slavoj Žižek, *In Defense of Lost Causes*, London: Verso, 2008, p. 95 et sqq.
6 Philippe Lacoue-Labarthe, *Heidegger, Art, and Politics: The Fiction of the Political*, Oxford: Blackwell, 1990.
7 Peter Sloterdijk, 'Heidegger's Politics: Postponing the End of History', in *What Happened in the Twentieth Century?*

17 Against negotiators and normative philosophers

1 The figure of the philosopher as 'conceptual negotiator' is proposed by Roberto Casati in his *Prima lezione di filosofia*, Bari: Laterza 2011.
2 Ibid., p. 57.
3 David Edmonds, *Would You Kill the Fat Man? The Trolley Problem and What Your Answer Tells Us*, Princeton: Princeton University Press, 2015.
4 See Donatella Di Cesare, *Torture*, Cambridge: Polity Press, 2018.
5 See John Rawls, *A Theory of Justice*, Cambridge, MA: Harvard University Press, 2009.
6 Alain Badiou and Slavoj Žižek, *Philosophy in the Present*, Cambridge: Polity Press, 2010.

18 *Ancilla democratiae*: a dejected return

1 Hannah Arendt, *The Origins of Totalitarianism*, London: Allen and Unwin, 1958.
2 Richard Rorty, 'The Priority of Democracy over Philosophy', in *Objectivity, Relativism and Truth: Philosophical Papers*, Cambridge: Cambridge University Press, 1991.
3 Hannah Arendt, *Lectures on Kant's Political Philosophy*, Chicago: University of Chicago Press, 1982.
4 A wide-ranging critique is advanced by Miguel Abensour, *Hannah Arendt contre la philosophie politique?*, Paris: Sens & Tonka, 2006. See also Alain Badiou, *Metapolitics*, London: Verso, 2012, and Slavoj Žižek, *The Ticklish Subject: The Absent Centre of Political Ontology*, London: Verso, 2009.
5 Jacques Rancière, *Disagreement: Politics and Philosophy*, Minneapolis: University of Minnesota Press, 2008.

19 The poetry of clarity

1 Dante Alighieri, 'De vulgari eloquentia', ed. P.V. Mengaldo, in *Opere minori*, Milan: Ricciardi, 1979.
2 Coluccio Salutati, *De laboribus Herculis*, ed. B.L. Ullmann, Turici: In aedibus Thesauri Mundi, 1951, I, p. 44; see also *Epistolario di Coluccio Salutati*, ed. F. Novati, IV, Rome: Istituto Storico Italiano-Forzani & Co, 1905, p. 177.

3 Giambattista Vico, *The New Science*, trans. Thomas Goddard Bergin and Max Harold Fisch, Ithaca: Cornell University Press, 1948.

20 Potent prophecies of the leap: Marx and Kierkegaard

1 Remo Bodei, *La civetta e la talpa. Sistema ed epoca in Hegel*, Bologna: il Mulino, 2018.
2 G.W.F. Hegel, *Elements of the Philosophy of Right*, Cambridge: Cambridge University Press, 1991.
3 Jacob Taubes, *Occidental Eschatology*, Stanford: Stanford University Press, 2009.
4 Karl Löwith, *From Hegel to Nietzsche: The Revolution in Nineteenth-Century Thought*, London: Constable and Co., 1965.
5 Karl Marx, 'Theses on Feuerbach', text from marxists.org.
6 Ernst Bloch, 'Changing the World: Marx's Theses on Feuerbach', in *On Karl Marx*, New York: Herder and Herder, 1971.
7 Karl Marx, 'A Contribution to the Critique of Hegel's Philosophy of Right', Introduction, text from marxists.org.
8 Ibid.
9 Taubes, *Occidental Eschatology*, p. 186.
10 Karl Marx, *Capital*, Vol. 1, 'Preface to the first German edition', text from marxists.org.
11 Søren Kierkegaard, *Either/Or*, Princeton: Princeton University Press, 1987, I, p. 16.
12 Ibid., p. 42.
13 Ibid., p. 26.
14 Taubes, *Occidental Eschatology*, p. 166.

21 The ecstasy of existence

1 See, for instance, Quentin Meillassoux, *After Finitude: An Essay on the Necessity of Contingency*, London: Bloomsbury, 2008.
2 See Graham Harman, *Object-Oriented Ontology: A New Theory of Everything*, London: Pelican Books 2018; *Speculative Realism: An Introduction*, Cambridge: Polity Press, 2018.
3 Martin Heidegger and Elisabeth Blochmann, *Briefwechsel 1918–1969*, Marbach am Neckar: Deutsches Literatur-Archiv, 1989.
4 Heidegger, *Being and Time*, §9.
5 Martin Heidegger, 'Letter on Humanism', in *Basic Writings:*

Nine Key Essays, plus the Introduction to Being and Time, trans. David Farrell Krell, London: Routledge, 1978.

6 Martin Heidegger, 'Die Metaphysik des deutschen Idealismus. Zur erneuten Auslegung von Schelling: Philosophische Untersuchungen über das Wesen der menschlichen Freiheit und die damit zusammenhängenden Gegenstände', *GA*, XLIX, 2, ed. G. Seubold, Frankfurt: Klostermann, 1991. Here, Heidegger comments on Kierkegaard's conceptions.

22 For an exophilia

1 Friedrich Nietzsche, *Thus Spoke Zarathustra*, New York: Barnes & Noble Classics, 2007.

23 The philosophy of awakening

1 Walter Benjamin, *The Arcades Project*, Cambridge, MA: Belknap Press of Harvard University Press, 1999, p. 405.
2 Ibid, p. 391.
3 Ibid., p. 458.
4 Ibid., p. 212.
5 Ibid., pp. 456, 907.
6 Ibid., p. 389.
7 Ibid.
8 Ibid., p. 406.
9 Ibid., p. 205.

24 Fallen angels and rag-pickers

1 Walter Benjamin, 'The Outsider Makes His Mark', in *Walter Benjamin: Selected Writings*, II, 1927–1934, Cambridge, MA: Belknap Press of Harvard University Press, 1999, p. 310, translation modified.
2 Walter Benjamin, 'Zum Problem der Physiognomik und Vohersagung', *Gesammelte Schriften*, VI, Frankfurt: Suhrkamp, 1985, p. 91.

25 Anarchist postscript

1 Heidegger, *Being and Time*, p. 292.

2 Judith Butler, *Precarious Life: The Power of Mourning and Violence*, London: Verso, 2004.

3 With regard to the autonomy of the subject, Rawls – who shares this myth – speaks of the 'aristocracy of all'. See John Rawls, *Lectures on the History of Moral Philosophy*, Cambridge, MA: Harvard University Press, 2003.

4 M. Abensour, 'An-Archy Between Metapolitics and Politics' (2002), in *The Anarchist Turn*, ed. J. Blumenfeld, C. Bottici and S. Critchley, London: Pluto Press, 2013, pp. 80–97.

5 Levinas, *Otherwise than Being, or, Beyond Essence*, p. 156.

6 Emmanuel Levinas, 'Subjectivity as AnArchy', in *God, Death, and Time*, Stanford: Stanford University Press, 2000.

7 Levinas, *Otherwise than Being, or, Beyond Essence*, p. 194.

8 Reiner Schürmann, *Heidegger on Being and Acting: From Principles to Anarchy*, Bloomington: Indiana University Press, 1987. See also A. Martinengo, *Introduzione a Reiner Schürmann*, Rome: Meltemi, 2008.

9 Giorgio Agamben, *Creazione e anarchia. L'opera nell'età della religione capitalistica*, Vicenza: Neri Pozza, 2017, p. 95.

10 Schürmann, *Heidegger on Being and Acting*, p. 6.

11 Simon Critchley, *The Ethics of Deconstruction: Derrida and Levinas*, Edinburgh: Edinburgh University Press, 2014, p. 314.

12 Donatella Di Cesare, *Resident Foreigners: A Philosophy of Migration*, Cambridge: Polity Press, 2020.

Bibliography

Abensour, Miguel, 'An-Archy Between Metapolitics and Politics' (2002), in *The Anarchist Turn*, ed. Jacob Blumenfeld, Chiara Bottici and Simon Critchley, London: Pluto Press, 2013.

Abensour, Miguel, *Hannah Arendt contre la philosophie politique?*, Paris: Sens & Tonka, 2006.

Adorno, Theodor W., *Philosophische Terminologie*, Frankfurt: Suhrkamp, 1973.

Adorno, Theodor W., *Metaphysics: Concept and Problems*, Cambridge: Polity Press, 2015.

Agamben, Giorgio, *Che cos'è la filosofia?*, Macerata: Quodlibet, 2016.

Agamben, Giorgio, *Creazione e anarchia. L'opera nell'età della religione capitalistica*, Vicenza: Neri Pozza, 2017.

Alighieri, Dante, 'De vulgari eloquentia', ed. P.V. Mengaldo, in *Opere minori*, Milan: Ricciardi, 1979.

Arendt, Hannah, *The Origins of Totalitarianism*, London: Allen and Unwin, 1958.

Arendt, Hannah, 'Martin Heidegger at Eighty', *New York Review of Books*, 21 October 1971, pp. 50–4.

Arendt, Hannah, *The Life of the Mind*, Boston: Harcourt, 1981.

Arendt, Hannah, *Lectures on Kant's Political Philosophy*, Chicago: University of Chicago Press, 1982.

Arendt, Hannah, *Responsibility and Judgment*, New York: Schocken Books, 2005.

Arendt, Hannah, *Socrate*, Milan: Cortina, 2015.

Badiou, Alain, *Metapolitics*, London: Verso, 2012.

Badiou, Alain, *The Century*, Cambridge: Polity Press, 2018.

Badiou, Alain and Slavoj Žižek, *Philosophy in the Present*, Cambridge: Polity Press, 2010.

Benjamin, Walter, *The Arcades Project*, Cambridge, MA: Belknap Press of Harvard University Press, 1999.

Benjamin, Walter, 'The Outsider Makes His Mark', in *Walter Benjamin: Selected Writings*, II, 1927–1934, Cambridge, MA: Belknap Press of Harvard University Press, 1999.

Blanchot, Maurice, *The Writing of the Disaster*, Lincoln: University of Nebraska Press, 2015.

Bloch, Ernst, 'Tübinger Einleitung in die Philosophie' (1963), in *Werkausgabe*, XIII, Frankfurt: Suhrkamp, 1963.

Bloch, Ernst, 'Changing the World: Marx's Theses on Feuerbach', in *On Karl Marx*, New York: Herder and Herder, 1971.

Blumenberg, Hans, *Die Verführbarkeit des Philosophen*, ed. Manfred Sommer in collaboration with the Hans Blumenberg-Archiv, Frankfurt: Suhrkamp, 2000.

Blumenberg, Hans, *The Laughter of the Thracian Woman*, London: Bloomsbury, 2015.

Bodei, Remo, *La filosofia nel Novecento (e oltre)*, Milan: Feltrinelli, 2015.

Bodei, Remo, *La civetta e la talpa. Sistema ed epoca in Hegel*, Bologna: il Mulino, 2018.

Böhme, Gernot, *Der Typ Sokrates*, Frankfurt: Suhrkamp, 2002.

Bouveresse, Jacques, *La demande philosophique. Que veut la philosophie et que peut-on vouloir d'elle?*, Paris: L'Eclat, 1996.

Brancacci, Aldo, 'Socrate e il tema semantico della coscienza', in Gabriele Giannantoni and Michel Narcy (eds.), *Lezioni socratiche*, Naples: Bibliopolis, 1997.

Buber, Martin, *Logos. Zwei Reden*, Heidelberg: Lambert Schneider, 1962.

Butler, Judith, *Precarious Life: The Power of Mourning and Violence*, London: Verso, 2004.

Casati, Roberto, *Prima lezione di filosofia*, Bari: Laterza, 2011.

Cicero, Marcus Tullius, *Opere filosofiche*, trans. and ed. Nino Marinone, Turin: Utet, 2016.

Crary, Jonathan, *24/7: Late Capitalism and the Ends of Sleep*, London: Verso, 2013.

Critchley, Simon, *Infinitely Demanding: Ethics of Commitment, Politics of Resistance*, London: Verso, 2007.

Danowski, Déborah and Eduardo Batalha Viveiros de Castro, *The Ends of the World*, Cambridge: Polity Press, 2017.

Edmonds, David, *Would You Kill the Fat Man? The Trolley Problem and What Your Answer Tells Us*, Princeton: Princeton University Press, 2015.

Deleuze, Gilles and Félix Guattari, *What is Philosophy?*, New York: Columbia University Press, 1994.

Derrida, Jacques, *La carte postale: de Socrate à Freud at au-delà*, Paris: Flammarion, 1980.

Di Cesare, Donatella, *Heidegger and the Jews: The Black Notebooks*, Cambridge: Polity Press, 2018.

Di Cesare, Donatella, *Torture*, Cambridge: Polity Press, 2018.

Di Cesare, Donatella, *Resident Foreigners: A Philosophy of Migration*, Cambridge: Polity Press, 2020.

Diogenes Laërtius, *The Lives and Opinions of Eminent Philosophers*, London: G. Bell and Sons, 1915.

Esposito, Roberto, *Immunitas: The Protection and Negation of Life*, Cambridge: Polity Press, 2013.

Fisher, Mark, *Capitalist Realism: Is There No Alternative?*, Winchester: Zero Books, 2010.

Foucault, Michel, 'Of Other Spaces: Utopias and Heterotopias,' in *Rethinking Architecture: A Reader in Cultural Theory*, ed. Neil Leach, New York: Routledge, 1997.

Gadamer, Hans-Georg, 'Oberflächlichkeit und Unkenntnis. Zur Veröffentlichung von Victor Farias', in *Antwort: Martin Heidegger im Gespräch*, ed. Günther Neske and Emil Kettering, Pfullingen: Neske, 1988.

Habermas, Jürgen, 'Does Philosophy Still Have a Purpose' (1971), in *Philosophical-Political Profiles*, Cambridge: Polity Press, 2012.

Hadot, Pierre, *What is Ancient Philosophy?*, Cambridge, MA: Belknap Press, 2004.

Hampe, Michael, *Die Lehren der Philosophie. Eine Kritik*, Frankfurt: Suhrkamp, 2014.

Hardt, Michael and Antonio Negri, *Empire*, Cambridge, MA: Harvard University Press, 2000.

Harman, Graham, *Object-Oriented Ontology: A New Theory of Everything*, London: Pelican, 2018.

Harman, Graham, *Speculative Realism: An Introduction*, Cambridge: Polity Press, 2018.

Hegel, G.W.F., *Elements of the Philosophy of Right*, Cambridge: Cambridge University Press, 1991.

Hegel, G.W.F., *The Phenomenology of Spirit*, Notre Dame: University of Notre Dame Press, 2019.

Hegel, G.W.F., *Lectures on the History of Philosophy*, text from marxists.org.

Heidegger, Martin, *Being and Time*, Oxford: Blackwell, 1962.

Heidegger, Martin, *The Question Concerning Technology and Other Essays*, New York: Garland, 1977.

Heidegger, Martin, 'Letter on Humanism', in *Basic Writings: Nine Key Essays, plus the Introduction to Being and Time*, trans. David Farrell Krell, London: Routledge, 1978.

Heidegger, Martin, 'Die Metaphysik des deutschen Idealismus. Zur erneuten Auslegung von Schelling: Philosophische Untersuchungen über das Wesen der menschlichen Freiheit und die damit zusammenhängenden Gegenstände', *GA*, XLIX, 2, ed. G. Seubold, Frankfurt: Klostermann, 1991.

Heidegger, Martin, *What is That – Philosophy?* trans. Eva T.H. Brann, Annapolis: St. John's College, 1991.

Heidegger, Martin, *The Fundamental Concepts of Metaphysics: World, Finitude, Solitude*, Bloomington: Indiana University Press, 1995.

Heidegger, Martin, *Kant and the Problem of Metaphysics*, Bloomington: Indiana University Press, 1997.

Heidegger, Martin, 'Phänomenologische Interpretation zu Aristoteles' (1921–22), in *GA*, LXII, 2: *Phänomenologische Interpretation zu Aristoteles – Einführung in die phänomenologische Forschung*, ed. W. Bröcker and K. Bröcker-Oltmanns, Frankfurt: Klostermann, 2005.

Heidegger, Martin and Elisabeth Blochmann, *Briefwechsel 1918–1969*, Marbach am Neckar: Deutsches Literatur-Archiv, 1989.

Hersch, Jeanne, *L'étonnement philosophique: une histoire de la philosophie*, Paris: Gallimard, 2017.

Hobsbawm, Eric, *Age of Extremes: The Short Twentieth Century, 1914–1991*, New York: Viking, 1994.

Horkheimer, Max, 'The Social Function of Philosophy', Radical Philosophy 3:10, 1972, pp. 10–14.

Giannantoni, Gabriele (ed.), *I presocratici. Frammenti e testimonianze*, Bari: Laterza, 1975.

Jaspers, Karl, *Von der Wahrheit. Philosophische Logik*, Munich: R. Piper Verlag, 1947.

Jaspers, Karl, *Way to Wisdom: An Introduction to Philosophy*, New Haven: Yale University Press, 2003.

Kant, Immanuel, *Critique of Pure Reason*, New York: Macmillan, 1922.

Kant, Immanuel, *Prolegomena to Any Future Metaphysics*, trans. Jonathan Bennett, at https://www.earlymoderntexts.com/assets/pdfs/kant1783.pdf.

Kierkegaard, Søren, *Either/Or*, Princeton: Princeton University Press, 1987.

Lacoue-Labarthe, Philippe, *Heidegger, Art, and Politics: The Fiction of the Political*, Oxford: Blackwell, 1990.

Levinas, Emmanuel, *Otherwise than Being, or, Beyond Essence*, Boston: Dordrecht, 1991.

Lübbe, Hermann (ed.), *Wozu Philosophie? Stellungnahmen eines Arbeitskreises*, Berlin: De Gruyter, 2014.

Maier, Heinrich, *Sokrates, sein Werk und seine geschichtliche Stellung*, Darmstadt: Scienta Uerlag Aalen, 1964.

Martens, Ekkehard, *Der Faden der Ariadne oder Warum alle Philosophen spinnen*, Leipzig: Reclam, 2000.

Martinengo, Alberto, *Introduzione a Reiner Schürmann*, Rome: Meltemi, 2008.

Marx, Karl, 'A Contribution to the Critique of Hegel's Philosophy of Right', Introduction, text from marxists.org.

Marx, Karl, 'Theses on Feuerbach', text from marxists.org.

Marx, Karl, *Capital: A Critique of Political Economy*, Vol. I, London: Penguin, 1990.

Meillassoux, Quentin, *After Finitude: An Essay on the Necessity of Contingency*, London: Bloomsbury, 2008.

Merleau-Ponty, Maurice, *In Praise of Philosophy and Other Essays*, Evanston: Northwestern University Press, 1988.

Montaigne, Michel de, *Essays*, London: Arnold, 1971.

Neyrat, Frédéric, *Atopias: Manifesto for a Radical Existentialism*, New York: Fordham University Press, 2018.

Nietzsche, Friedrich, *The Gay Science. With a Prelude in Rhymes and an Appendix of Songs*, New York: Vintage Books, 1974.

Nietzsche, Friedrich, 'On Truth and Lies in a Nonmoral Sense', in *The Portable Nietzsche*, New York: Viking Press, 1976.

Nietzsche, Friedrich, *Thus Spoke Zarathustra*, New York: Barnes & Noble Classics, 2007.

Novalis, 'Hymnen an die Nacht' (1800), in *Werke*, ed. Gerhard Schulz, Munich: C.H. Beck, 1969.

Novalis, 'Aus dem "Allgemeinen Brouillon"', in *Werke*, ed. Gerhard Schulz, Munich: C.H. Beck, 1987.

Noys, Benjamin, *Malign Velocities: Acceleration and Capitalism*, Winchester: Zero Books, 2014.

Rancière, Jacques, *Disagreement: Politics and Philosophy*, Minneapolis: University of Minnesota Press, 2008.

Rawls, John, *Lectures on the History of Moral Philosophy*, Cambridge, MA: Harvard University Press, 2003.

Rawls, John, *A Theory of Justice*, Cambridge, MA: Harvard University Press, 2009.

Rilke, Rainer Maria, *Duino Elegies*, London: Hogarth Press, 1939.

Rorty, Richard, 'The Priority of Democracy over Philosophy', in *Objectivity, Relativism and Truth: Philosophical Papers*, Cambridge: Cambridge University Press, 1991.

Rosa, Hartmut, *Alienation and Acceleration: Towards a Critical Theory of Late Modern Temporality*, Aarhus: NSU Press, 2010.

Salutati, Coluccio, *Epistolario di Coluccio Salutati*, ed. F. Novati, IV, Rome: Istituto Storico Italiano-Forzani & Co, 1905.

Salutati, Coluccio, *De laboribus Herculis*, ed. B.L. Ullmann, Turici: In aedibus Thesauri Mundi, 1951.

Sassi, Maria Michela, *Indagine su Socrate. Persona, cittadino, filosofo*, Turin: Einaudi, 2015.

Schürmann, Reiner, *Heidegger on Being and Acting: From Principles to Anarchy*, Bloomington: Indiana University Press, 1987.

Sloterdijk, Peter, *Weltfremdheit*, Frankfurt: Suhrkamp, 1993.

Sloterdijk, Peter, *Scheintod im Denken: von Philosophie und Wissenschaft als Übung*, Berlin: Suhrkamp, 2012.

Sloterdijk, Peter, *Globes. Spheres Volume II: Macrospherology*, New York: semiotext(e), 2014.

Sloterdijk, Peter, 'The City and its Negation: An Outline of Negative Political Theory', in *The Aesthetic Imperative: Writings on Art*, New York: John Wiley & Sons, 2017.

Sloterdijk, Peter, *What Happened in the Twentieth Century? Towards a Critique of Extremist Reason*, Cambridge: Polity Press, 2018.

Stengers, Isabelle, *Au temps des catastrophes. Résister la barbarie qui vient*, Paris: La Découverte, 2013.

Stimilli, Elettra, *Jacob Taubes. Sovranità e tempo messianico*, Brescia: Morcelliana, 2004.

Strauss, Leo, *Jerusalem and Athens: Some Preliminary Reflections*, New York: City College, 1967.

Strauss, Leo, *What is Political Philosophy? And Other Studies*, Chicago: University of Chicago Press 2008.

Taubes, Jacob, *Occidental Eschatology*, Stanford: Stanford University Press, 2009.

Unger, Erich, *Politik und Metaphysik*, Würzburg: Königshausen & Neumann, 1989.

Vico, Giambattista, *The New Science*, trans. Thomas Goddard Bergin and Max Harold Fisch, Ithaca: Cornell University Press, 1948.

Vlastos, Gregory, *Socrates: Ironist and Moral Philosopher*, Ithaca: Cornell University Press, 1992.

Wittgenstein, Ludwig, *The Big Typescript*, Vienna: Springer, 2000.

Žižek, Slavoj, *In Defence of Lost Causes*, London: Verso, 2008.

Žižek, Slavoj, *The Ticklish Subject: The Absent Centre of Political Ontology*, London: Verso, 2009.

Žižek, Slavoj, *Demanding the Impossible*, Cambridge: Polity Press, 2013.

Index